ADORATION

Adoration

EUCHARISTIC
TEXTS AND PRAYERS
THROUGHOUT
CHURCH HISTORY

Compiled by
Daniel P. Guernsey

IGNATIUS PRESS   SAN FRANCISCO

Cover photograph © by Charlene Dorman
Corpus Christi Monastery
of the Nuns of the Order of Preachers
Menlo Park, California

Cover design by Roxanne Mei Lum

© 1999 Ignatius Press, San Francisco
All rights reserved
ISBN 0-89870-670-x
Library of Congress catalogue number 97-76850
Printed in the United States of America ∞

Contents

Introduction

The Church and the world have a great need of eucharistic worship. Jesus waits for us in this sacrament of love. Let us be generous with our time in going to meet Him in adoration and in contemplation that is full of faith and ready to make reparation for the great faults and crimes of the world. May our adoration never cease.

— Pope John Paul II, *Dominicae Cenae*

These eucharistic texts and prayers from throughout the history of the Church are presented in an effort to aid and promote the adoration of the Blessed Sacrament. This compilation is not even remotely exhaustive of the inspirational and beautiful eucharistic texts the Church possesses. They are simply a few representative texts that may aid the worshipper in increasing devotion to this most Blessed of Sacraments.

Acknowledgments

The author and publisher gratefully acknowledge the following for their kind permission to reprint selections from their copyrighted works:

Oxford University Press, Oxford and New York, for *The Early Christian Fathers*, ed. by Henry Bettenson, © 1956; *The Later Christian Fathers*, ed. by Henry Bettenson, © 1970; *Saint Thomas Aquinas: Theological Texts*, ed. by Thomas Gilby, © 1955.

Alba House, Staten Island, N.Y., for *The Mass: Ancient Liturgies and Patristic Texts*, ed. by Adalbert Hamman, O.F.M., © 1969.

Montfort Publications, Bay Shore, N.Y., for *True Devotion to the Blessed Virgin*, by Saint Louis de Montfort, © 1991.

Servant Publications, Ann Arbor, Mich., for *Mother Teresa: Total Surrender*, ed. by Brother Angelo Devananda, © 1985; *One Heart Full of Love*, by Mother Teresa, © 1984.

Costello Publishing Company, Northport, N.Y., for *Vatican Council II, The Conciliar and Post Conciliar Documents*, ed. by Austin Flannery, O.P., © 1984, Costello Publishing Company, Northport, N.Y. Excerpts are used by permission of the publisher, all rights reserved. No part of these excerpts may be reproduced, stored in a retrieval system, or transmitted in any form or by any means—electronic, mechanical, photo-copying, recording or otherwise, without express permission of Costello Publishing Company.

Apostolate for Perpetual Adoration, West Covina, Calif., for *Loving Jesus with the Heart of Mary (Fifteen Eucharistic Meditations on the Fifteen Mysteries of the Rosary)*, by Martin Lucia, SS.CC., © 1985.

Tan Books and Publishers, Rockford, Ill., for *A Prayerbook of Favorite Litanies*, ed. by Albert Herbert, © 1985.

Catholic Book Publishing Co., New York, for *Treasury of Novenas*, ed. by Lawrence Lovasik, S.V.D., © 1986.

Source Books, Trabuco Canyon, Calif., for *Eucharistic Meditations*, by Saint John Vianney, ed. by Abbé H. Convert, trans. by Sr. Mary Benvenuta O.P., © 1993.

Redemptorist Fathers, Brooklyn, N.Y., for *The Holy Eucharist*, by Saint Alphonsus Liguori, © 1934.

Emmanuel Publications, Cleveland, Ohio, for *Eucharistic Handbook*, by Saint Peter Julian Eymard, © 1948.

Scepter Publishers, Princeton, N.J., for *The Way*, by Blessed Josemaría Escrivá, © 1982.

Confraternity of the Precious Blood, Brooklyn, N.Y., for *My Daily Bread*, by A.J. Paone, © 1954.

The United States Catholic Conference, Washington, D.C., for *Catechism of the Catholic Church*, © 1994.

The Congregation of Marians of the Immaculate Conception, Stockbridge, Mass., for *Divine Mercy in My Soul: Diary of Sr. M. Faustina Kowalska*, by Sr. Faustina Kowalska. Reprinted by permission of the Congregation of Marians of the Immaculate Conception. All world rights reserved. © 1987.

The Canon Law Society, Washington, D.C., for *The Code of Canon Law*, © 1983.

Scripture quotations are from the Revised Standard Version of the Bible, copyright 1946, 1952, and 1957; Catholic Edition copyright 1965, 1966 by the Division of Christian Education of the National Council of the Churches of Christ in the United States of America. Used by permission.

EUCHARISTIC TEXTS

FROM THE NEW TESTAMENT

Then came the day of Unleavened Bread, on which the passover lamb had to be sacrificed. So Jesus sent Peter and John, saying, "Go and prepare the passover for us, that we may eat it." They said to him, "Where will you have us prepare it?" He said to them, "Behold, when you have entered the city, a man carrying a jar of water will meet you; follow him into the house which he enters, and tell the householder, 'The Teacher says to you, Where is the guest room, where I am to eat the passover with my disciples?' And he will show you a large upper room furnished; there make ready." And they went, and found it as he had told them; and they prepared the passover.

And when the hour came, he sat at table, and the apostles with him. And he said to them, "I have earnestly desired to eat this passover with you before I suffer; for I tell you I shall not eat it until it is fulfilled in the kingdom of God." And he took a cup, and when he had given thanks he said, "Take this, and divide it among yourselves; for I tell you that from now on I shall not drink of the fruit of the vine until the kingdom of God comes." And he took bread, and when he had given thanks he broke it and gave it to them, saying, "This is my body, which is given for you. Do this in remembrance of me." And likewise the cup after supper, saying, "This cup which is poured out for you is the new covenant in my blood."[1]

And as they were eating, he took bread, and blessed, and broke it, and gave it to them, and said, "Take; this is my body." And he took a cup, and when he had given thanks he gave it to them, and they all drank of it. And he said to them, "This is my blood of the covenant, which is poured out for many."[2]

Now as they were eating, Jesus took bread, and blessed, and broke it, and gave it to the disciples and said, "Take, eat; this is my body." And he took a cup, and when he had given thanks he gave it to them, saying, "Drink of it, all of you; for this is my blood of the covenant, which is poured out for many for the forgiveness of sins."[3]

When they [the crowd after the multiplication of the loaves] found him on the other side of the sea, they said to him, "Rabbi, when did you come here?" Jesus answered them, "Truly, truly, I say to you, you seek me, not because you saw signs, but because you ate your fill of the loaves. Do not labor for the food which perishes, but for the food which endures to eternal life, which the Son of man will give to you; for on him has God the Father set his seal." Then they said to him, "What must we do, to be doing the works of God?" Jesus answered them, "This is the work of God, that you believe in him whom he has sent." So they said to him, "Then what sign do you do, that we may see, and believe you? What work do you perform? Our fathers ate manna in the wilderness; as it is written, 'He gave them bread from heaven to eat.'" Jesus then said to them, "Truly, truly, I say to you, it was not Moses who gave you the bread from heaven; my Father gives you the true bread from heaven. For the bread of God is that which comes down from heaven, and gives life to the world." They said to him, "Lord, give us this bread always."

Jesus said to them, "I am the bread of life; he who comes to me shall not hunger, and he who believes in me shall never thirst. But I said to you that you have seen me and yet do not believe. All that the Father gives me will come to me; and him who comes to me I will not cast out. For I have come down from heaven, not to do my own will, but the will of him who sent me; and this is the will of him who sent me, that I should lose nothing of all that he has given me, but raise it up at the last day. For this is the will of my Father, that every one who sees the Son and believes in him should have eternal life; and I will raise him up at the last day."

The Jews then murmured at him, because he said, "I am the bread which came down from heaven." They said, "Is not this Jesus, the son of Joseph, whose father and mother we know? How does he now say, 'I have come down from heaven'?" Jesus answered them, "Do not murmur among yourselves. No one can come to me unless the Father who sent me draws him; and I will raise him up at the last day. It is written in the prophets, 'And they shall all be taught by God.' Every one who has heard and learned from the Father comes to me. Not that any one has seen the Father except him who is from God; he has seen the Father. Truly,

truly, I say to you, he who believes has eternal life. I am the bread of life. Your fathers ate the manna in the wilderness, and they died. This is the bread which comes down from heaven, that a man may eat of it and not die. I am the living bread which came down from heaven; if any one eats of this bread, he will live for ever; and the bread which I shall give for the life of the world is my flesh.''

The Jews then disputed among themselves, saying, ''How can this man give us his flesh to eat?'' So Jesus said to them, ''Truly, truly, I say to you, unless you eat the flesh of the Son of man and drink his blood, you have no life in you; he who eats my flesh and drinks my blood has eternal life, and I will raise him up at the last day. For my flesh is food indeed, and my blood is drink indeed. He who eats my flesh and drinks my blood abides in me, and I in him. As the living Father sent me, and I live because of the Father, so he who eats me will live because of me. This is the bread which came down from heaven, not such as the fathers ate and died; he who eats this bread will live for ever.'' This he said in the synagogue, as he taught at Capernaum.

Many of his disciples, when they heard it, said, ''This is a hard saying; who can listen to it?'' But Jesus, knowing in himself that his disciples murmured at it, said to them, ''Do you take offense at this? Then what if you were to see the Son of man ascending where he was before? It is the spirit that gives life, the flesh is of no avail; the words that I have spoken to you are spirit and life. But there are some of you that do not believe." For Jesus knew from the first who those were that did not believe, and who it was that should betray him. And he said, "This is why I told you that no one can come to me unless it is granted him by the Father."

After this many of his disciples drew back and no longer went about with him. Jesus said to the twelve, "Will you also go away?" Simon Peter answered him, "Lord, to whom shall we go? You have the words of eternal life; and we have believed, and have come to know, that you are the Holy One of God." [4]

[After two disciples encounter a "stranger" on the road to Emmaus:]

So they drew near to the village to which they were going. He [the risen Christ] appeared to be going further, but they constrained him, saying, "Stay with us, for it is toward evening and the day is now far spent." So he went in to stay with them. When he was at table with them, he took the bread and blessed, and broke it, and gave it to them. And their eyes were opened and they recognized him; and he vanished out of their sight. They said to each other, "Did not our hearts burn within us while he talked to us on the road, while he opened to us the scriptures?" And they rose that same hour and returned to Jerusalem; and they found the eleven gathered together and those who were with them, who said, "The Lord has risen indeed, and has appeared to Simon!" Then they told what had happened on the road, and how he was known to them in the breaking of the bread. [5]

So if you are offering your gift at the altar, and there remember that your brother has something against you,
leave your gift there before the altar and go; first be
reconciled to your brother, and then come and offer
your gift.[6]

The cup of blessing which we bless, is it not a participation in the blood of Christ? The bread which we
break, is it not a participation in the body of Christ?
Because there is one bread, we who are many are one
body, for we all partake of the one bread.[7]

But in the following instructions I do not commend
you, because when you come together it is not for
the better but for the worse. For, in the first place,
when you assemble as a church, I hear that there are
divisions among you; and I partly believe it, for there
must be factions among you in order that those who
are genuine among you may be recognized. When you
meet together, it is not the Lord's supper that you eat.
For in eating, each one goes ahead with his own meal,
and one is hungry and another is drunk. What! Do
you not have houses to eat and drink in? Or do you
despise the church of God and humiliate those who
have nothing? What shall I say to you? Shall I commend you in this? No, I will not.

For I received from the Lord what I also delivered
to you, that the Lord Jesus on the night when he was
betrayed took bread, and when he had given thanks,
he broke it, and said, "This is my body which is for
you. Do this in remembrance of me." In the same way

also the cup, after supper, saying, "This cup is the new covenant in my blood. Do this, as often as you drink it, in remembrance of me." For as often as you eat this bread and drink the cup, you proclaim the Lord's death until he comes.

Whoever, therefore, eats the bread or drinks the cup of the Lord in an unworthy manner will be guilty of profaning the body and blood of the Lord. Let a man examine himself, and so eat of the bread and drink of the cup. For any one who eats and drinks without discerning the body eats and drinks judgment upon himself. That is why many of you are weak and ill, and some have died. But if we judged ourselves truly, we should not be judged. But when we are judged by the Lord, we are chastened so that we may not be condemned along with the world.

So then, my brethren, when you come together to eat, wait for one another—if any one is hungry, let him eat at home—lest you come together to be condemned. About the other things I will give directions when I come.[8]

THE EUCHARIST PREFIGURED
IN THE OLD TESTAMENT

Then Moses called all the elders of Israel, and said to them, "Select lambs for yourselves according to your families, and kill the passover lamb. Take a bunch of hyssop and dip it in the blood which is in the basin, and touch the lintel and the two doorposts with the blood which is in the basin; and none of you shall go out of the door of his house until the morning. For the Lord will pass through to slay the Egyptians; and when he sees the blood on the lintel and on the two doorposts, the Lord will pass over the door, and will not allow the destroyer to enter your houses to slay you. You shall observe this rite as an ordinance for you and for your sons for ever. And when you come to the land which the Lord will give you, as he has promised, you shall keep this service. And when your children say to you, 'What do you mean by this service?' you shall say, 'It is the sacrifice of the Lord's passover, for he passed over the houses of the people of Israel in Egypt, when he slew the Egyptians but spared our houses.' " [9]

The Lord said to Moses and Aaron in the land of Egypt, "This month shall be for you the beginning of months; it shall be the first month of the year for you. Tell all the congregation of Israel that on the tenth day of this month they shall take every man a lamb according to their fathers' houses, a lamb for a household; and if the household is too small for a lamb, then a man and his neighbor next to his house shall take according to the number of persons; according to what each can eat you shall make your count for the lamb. Your lamb shall be without blemish, a male a year old; you shall take it from the sheep or from the goats; and you shall keep it until the fourteenth day of this month, when the whole assembly of the congregation of Israel shall kill their lambs in the evening. Then they shall take

some of the blood, and put it on the two doorposts
and the lintel of the houses in which they eat them.
They shall eat the flesh that night, roasted; with unleavened bread and bitter herbs they shall eat it.[10]

And the whole congregation of the people of Israel
murmured against Moses and Aaron in the wilderness,
and said to them, "Would that we had died by the
hand of the LORD in the land of Egypt, when we sat
by the fleshpots and ate bread to the full; for you have
brought us out into this wilderness to kill this whole
assembly with hunger."

Then the LORD said to Moses, "Behold, I will rain
bread from heaven for you; and the people shall go out
and gather a day's portion every day, that I may prove
them, whether they will walk in my law or not. . . ."

Now the house of Israel called its name manna; it
was like coriander seed, white, and the taste of it was
like wafers made with honey. And Moses said, "This
is what the LORD has commanded: 'Let an omer of it
be kept throughout your generations, that they may
see the bread with which I fed you in the wilderness,
when I brought you out of the land of Egypt.'" And
Moses said to Aaron, "Take a jar, and put an omer
of manna in it, and place it before the LORD, to be
kept throughout your generations." As the LORD commanded Moses, so Aaron placed it before the testimony, to be kept. And the people of Israel ate the
manna forty years, till they came to a habitable land.[11]

SAINT IGNATIUS OF ANTIOCH

(Bishop of Antioch, martyred c. 115)

Therefore be eager for more frequent gatherings for thanksgiving [eucharist] to God and for his glory. For when you meet frequently the forces of Satan are annulled and his destructive power is canceled in the concord of your faith. [12]

Meet together in common—every single one of you—in grace, in one faith and one Jesus Christ (who was of David's line in his human nature, son of man and son of God) that you may obey the bishop and presbytery with undistracted mind; breaking one bread, which is the medicine of immortality, our antidote to ensure that we shall not die but live in Jesus Christ for ever. [13]

[While on his way to martyrdom:]

I die for Christ of my own choice, unless you hinder me. I beseech you not to show "inopportune kindness" to me. Let me be given to the wild beasts, for by their means I can attain God. I am God's wheat, and am being ground by the teeth of beasts so that I may appear as pure bread. . . . Entreat the Lord for me that through these instruments I may appear as a sacrifice to God. . . . I write to you while alive, yet longing for death; my desire has been crucified and there is not in me any sensuous fire, but living water bound up in me, and saying inside me, "Come to the Father." I have no pleasure in food which is destined for corruption, nor in the delights of this life. I desire the bread of God, which is the flesh of Christ who was of the seed of David; and for drink I desire his blood, which is incorruptible love.[14]

Take great care to keep one Eucharist. For there is one flesh of our Lord Jesus Christ and one cup to unite us by his blood; one sanctuary, as there is one bishop, together with the presbytery and the deacons, my fellow servants. Thus all your acts may be done according to God's will.[15]

They [the heretics] have no concern for love, none for the widow, the orphan, the afflicted, the prisoner, the hungry, the thirsty. They stay away from Eucharist and prayer, because they do not admit that the Eucharist is the flesh of our Savior Jesus Christ which suffered for our sins, which the Father raised up by his goodness.[16]

Shun divisions, as the beginning of evils. All of you follow the bishop, as Jesus Christ followed the Father, and the presbytery as the Apostles; respect the deacons as the ordinance of God. Let no one do anything that pertains to the church apart from the bishop. Let that be considered a valid Eucharist which is under the bishop or one whom he has delegated. Wherever the bishop shall appear, there let the people be; just as wherever Christ Jesus may be, there is the catholic Church. It is not permitted to baptize or hold an agape [Eucharist] independently of the bishop. But whatever he approves, that is also well-pleasing to God; that all your acts may be sure and valid.[17]

THE DIDACHĒ

(c. First or Second Century)

Give thanks in this manner. First, over the cup: "We give thanks to thee, our Father, for the holy vine of thy son David, which thou hast made known to us through Jesus thy Son: Thine be the glory forever." Then over the broken bread: "We give thanks to thee, our Father, for the life and knowledge which thou didst make known to us through Jesus thy Son: Thine be the glory forever. As this broken bread was scattered upon the mountains and was gathered together and became one, so let thy Church be gathered together from the ends of the earth into thy kingdom: for thine is the power and the glory through Jesus Christ forever and ever."

Let none eat or drink of this Eucharist of yours except those who have been baptized into the name of the Lord. For on this point the Lord said, "Do not give what is holy to the dogs."[18]

On the Lord's Day assemble together and break bread and give thanks, first making public confession of your faults, that your sacrifice may be pure. If any man has a quarrel with a friend, let him not join your assembly until they are reconciled, that your sacrifice may not be defiled. For this is the sacrifice spoken of by the Lord: "In every place and time offer me a pure sacrifice. . . ."[19]

SAINT JUSTIN MARTYR
(Martyred c. 165)

At the end of prayers we embrace each other with a kiss. Then the bread is brought to the president of the brethren, and a cup of water and wine: this he takes, and offers praise and glory to the Father of all, through the name of his Son and of the Holy Spirit; and he gives thanks at length for our being granted these gifts at hand. When he has finished the prayers and the thanksgiving [Eucharist] all the people present give their assent with *Amen*, a Hebrew word signifying "So be it". When the president has given thanks [or celebrated the Eucharist] and all the people have assented, those whom we call "deacons" give a portion of the bread over which the thanksgiving has been offered, and of the wine and water, to each of those who are present; and they carry them away to those who are absent.[20]

This food is called Eucharist [thanksgiving] with us, and only those are allowed to partake who believe in the truth of our teaching and have received the washing for the remission of sins and for regeneration; and who live in accordance with the directions of Christ. We do not receive these gifts as ordinary food or ordinary drink. But as Jesus Christ our Savior who was made flesh through the word of God, and took flesh and blood for our salvation; in the same way the food over which thanksgiving has been offered through the word of prayer which we have from him—the food by which our blood and flesh are nourished through its transformation—is, we are taught, the flesh and blood of Jesus who was made flesh.[21]

SAINT IRENAEUS OF LYONS
(Bishop of Lyons, 202)

Only the Catholic Church can offer to God the sacrifice which is pleasing to him, announced by the prophets, namely the sacrifice of the Eucharist. It utilizes the products of creation, bread, and wine which, contrary to the allegations of the Gnostics, is good. These elements are consecrated by the Church by the words of Christ as handed down in tradition.[22]

For it behooves us to make an oblation to God, and in all things to be found grateful to God our Maker, in a pure mind, and in faith without hypocrisy, in well grounded hope, in fervent love, offering the first fruits of his own created things. And the Church alone offers this pure oblation to the Creator, offering to him, with giving of thanks, [the things taken] from his creation.[23]

And just as a cutting from the vine planted in the ground fructifies in its season, or as a corn of wheat falling into the earth and becoming decomposed, rises with manifold increase by the Spirit of God, who contains all things, and then, through the wisdom of God, serves for the use of men, and having received the

Word of God, becomes the Eucharist, which is the body and blood of Christ; so also our bodies, being nourished by it, and deposited in the earth, and suffering decomposition there, shall rise at the appointed time, the Word of God granting them resurrection to the glory of God, even the Father, who freely "gives to this mortal immortality, and to this corruptible incorruption" (1 Cor 15:53), because the "strength of God is made perfect in weakness" (2 Cor 12:9).[24]

How can they [the heretics who deny bodily resurrection] say that the flesh passes to corruption and does not share in life, seeing that the flesh is nourished by the body and blood of the Lord? Let them either change their opinion, or refrain from making the oblations of which we have been speaking. But our opinion [of bodily resurrection] is congruous with the Eucharist, and the Eucharist supports our opinion. We offer to him [God] what is our own, suitably proclaiming the communion and unity of flesh and spirit. For as the bread, which comes from the earth, receives the invocation of God, and then is no longer common bread but Eucharist, consists of two things, an earthly and a heavenly; so our bodies after partaking of the Eucharist, are no longer corruptible, having the hope of eternal resurrection.[25]

We are his [Christ's] members, and are nourished by means of his creation (and he himself provides his creation for us, "making the sun to rise and sending rain as he wills"); therefore the drink, which is part of his creation, he declared to be his own blood; and the bread, which comes from his own creation, he affirmed to be his own body; and by this he nourishes our bodies. Whenever the cup that man mixes and the bread that man makes receive the word of God, the Eucharist becomes the body of Christ and by these elements the substance of our flesh receives nourishment and sustenance.[26]

MELITO OF SARDIS
(Monk, Second Century)

He came on earth from heaven for suffering man, becoming incarnate in a virgin's womb from which he came forth as man; he took on himself the sufferings of suffering man through a body capable of suffering, and put to an end the sufferings of the flesh, and through his spirit incapable of death he became the death of death which is destructive of man.

For led like a lamb, and slaughtered like a sheep, he ransomed us from the slavery of the world of Egypt, and loosened us from the slavery of the devil as from the hand of Pharaoh, and sealed our souls with his own spirit, and our bodily members with his own blood.

This is the one who covered death with the garment of reproach, who put the devil in mourning garb as Moses did Pharaoh. This is he who smote lawlessness and rendered injustice bereft of children as Moses did Egypt.

This is the one who rescued us from slavery to liberty, from darkness to light, from tyranny to the kingdom of eternity (who made us a new priesthood, a people chosen, eternal).

This is he who is the Passover of our salvation; this is he who suffered many things in many men. This is he who in Abel was slaughtered, in Jacob was exiled, in Joseph was sold, in Moses was exposed, in the lamb was immolated, in David was persecuted, in the prophets was maltreated. This is he in whom the virgin was made incarnate, on the cross was suspended, in the earth was buried, from the dead was resurrected, to the highest of heaven was lifted up.

This is the lamb without voice, this is the lamb slaughtered, this is the lamb born of the fair ewe, this is he who was taken from the flock, and dragged to immolation, and at evening slaughtered, and by night buried.

This is he who on the cross was not broken, and in the earth did not decay, but from the dead rose again, and raised up man from the depths of the tomb.[27]

TERTULLIAN

(c. 200)

The flesh feeds on the body and blood of Christ that the soul may be fattened on God.[28]

Many people think that they ought not to take part in the prayers of sacrifice [Eucharist] on station days [fast days], on the ground that the fast must be broken by reception of the Lord's body. Are we to suppose that the Eucharist cancels a devotion vowed to God? Does it not rather bind it to God? Will not your fast be more solemn if you have stood at God's altar? When the Lord's body has been received and reserved both points are secured—participation in the sacrifice and performance of the duty.[29]

SAINT CYPRIAN OF CARTHAGE
(Bishop of Carthage, 258)

But if it is not allowed to break the least of the commandments of the Lord, how much more important is it not to infringe upon matters which are so great, so tremendous, so closely connected to the very sacrament of the passion of the Lord and of our redemption, or in any way for human tradition to change what has been divinely instituted? For, if Christ Jesus, our Lord and God, is himself the High Priest of God the Father, and first offered himself as a sacrifice to his Father and commanded this to be done in commemoration of himself, certainly the priest who imitates that which Christ did and then offers the true and full sacrifice in the Church of God the Father, if he thus begins to offer according to what he sees Christ himself offered, performs truly in the place of Christ.[30]

And since we make mention of his passion in all sacrifices, for the passion of the Lord is, indeed, the sacrifice which we offer, we ought to do nothing other than what he did. For scripture says that, as often as we offer the chalice in the commemoration of the Lord and his passion (1 Cor 11:26), we should do that which it is certain the Lord did.[31]

If Christ Jesus, our Lord and God, is himself the high priest of God the Father, and commanded this to be done in remembrance of himself, then assuredly the priest acts truly in Christ's stead, when he reproduces what Christ did, and he then offers a true and complete sacrifice to God the Father.[32]

SAINT ATHANASIUS
(Bishop of Alexandria, 296–373)

My beloved brethren, it is not a temporal feast that we come to, but an eternal, heavenly feast. We do not display it in shadows; we approach it in reality. The Jews had their fill of the flesh of a dumb lamb, and when their feast was finished they anointed their door-posts with the blood, to beg for aid against the destroyer. But the food that we partake of is the Father's Word; we have the lintels of our hearts sealed with the blood of the new covenant; and we acknowledge the grace bestowed on us from our Savior.[33]

SAINT JOHN CHRYSOSTOM
(Bishop of Constantinople, 350)

Why can it have been that he ordained this sacrament, then, at the time of the Passover? That you might learn from everything, both that he is the lawgiver of the Old Testament, and that the things therein are fore-shadowed because of these things. Therefore, I say, where the type is, there he puts the truth.

Hence he shows that he is soon to die, wherefore also he made mention of a "Covenant", and he reminds them also of the former Covenant, for that also was dedicated with blood. Again he tells of the cause of his death, "which is shed for many for the remission of sins"; and he adds, "Do this in remembrance of me." See how he removes and draws them off the Jewish customs. For just as you did that, he says, in remembrance of the miracles in Egypt, so do this likewise in remembrance of me. That was shed for the preservation of the first-born, this for the remission of the sins of the whole world. "For this," said he, "is my blood, which is shed for the remission of sins." . . . And just as Moses says, "This shall be to you an everlasting memorial," so he says too, "in remembrance of me, until I come." Therefore, he also says, "With desire I have desired to eat this Passover," that is, to deliver you to the new rites, and to give a Passover, by which I am to make you spiritual.[34]

Let us then in everything believe God, and gainsay him nothing, though what is said seems to be contrary to our thoughts and senses, but let his word be of higher authority than both reasoning and sight. Thus let us do in the mysteries also, not looking at the things set before us, but keeping in mind his sayings.

For his word cannot deceive, but our senses are easily beguiled. His word never failed, but our senses in most things go wrong. Since then the word says, "This is my body," let us both be persuaded and believe, and look at it with the eyes of the mind.

For Christ has given nothing sensible, but though in things sensible yet all to be perceived by the mind. So also in baptism; the gift is bestowed by a sensible thing, that is, by water; but that which is done is perceived by the mind, the birth, I mean, and the renewal. For if you had been incorporeal, he would have delivered you the incorporeal gifts bare; but because the soul has been locked up in a body, he delivers you the things that the mind perceives, in things sensible.

How many now say, I would wish to see his form, his face, his clothes, his shoes? Lo! you see him. And you indeed desire to see his clothes, but he gives himself not to see only, but also to touch and eat and receive within you.[35]

Consider how indignant you are against the traitor, against them that crucified him. Look therefore, lest you also yourself become guilty of the body and blood of Christ. They slaughtered the all-holy body, but you receive it in a filthy soul after such great benefits.

Consider with what sort of honor you were honored, of what sort of table you are partaking. That which when angels behold, they tremble, and dare not so much as look up at it without awe on account of the brightness that comes thence, with this we are fed, with this we are commingled, and we are made one body and one flesh with Christ.[36]

"Who shall declare the mighty works of the Lord, and cause his praises to be heard?" (Ps 106:2) What shepherd feeds his sheep with his own limbs? And why do I say shepherd? There are often mothers that after the travail of birth send out their children to other women as nurses, but he endures not to do this; but himself feeds us with his own blood, and by all means entwines us with himself.[37]

The works set before us are not of man's power. He then did these things at that supper, this same now also works in them. We occupy the place of servants. He who sanctifies and changes them is the same. Let then no Judas be present, no covetous man. If anyone be not a disciple, let him withdraw, the table receives not such. For "I keep the Passover," he says, "with my disciples."

This table is the same as that, and has nothing less. For it is not so that Christ wrought that, and man this, but he does this too.[38]

Let us, then, come back from that table like lions breathing out fire, thus becoming terrifying to the

Devil, and remaining mindful of our Head and of the love that he has shown us.[39]

"Parents, it is true, often entrust their children to others to be fed, but I do not do so," he says; "I nourish mine on my own flesh. I give myself to you, since I desire all of you to be of noble birth, and I hold out to you fair hopes for the future. He who gives himself to you here will do so much more in the life to come. I wished to become your brother. When for your sake I had assumed flesh and blood, I gave back again to you that very flesh and blood through which I had become your kinsman." This blood makes the seal of our King bright in us; it produces an inconceivable beauty; it does not permit the nobility of the soul to become corrupt, since it refreshes and nourishes it without ceasing.[40]

The blood which we receive by way of food is not immediately a source of nourishment, but goes through some other stage first; this is not so with this blood, for it at once refreshes the soul and instills a certain great power in it. This blood, when worthily received, drives away demons and puts them at a distance from us, and even summons to us angels and the Lord of angels. Where they see the blood of the Lord, demons flee, while angels gather. This blood, poured out in abundance, has washed the whole world clean. The blessed Paul has uttered many truths about this blood in the Epistle to the Hebrews (cf. Heb 9). This blood has purified the sanctuary and the holy of holies.[41]

Now, if its type had so much power, both in the Temple of the Hebrews and in the midst of the Egyptians, when sprinkled on the doorposts (cf. Ex 12, 7, 13), much more power does the reality have. In its types this blood sanctified the golden altar; without it, the high priest did not dare to enter the sanctuary. This blood has ordained priests; in its types it has washed away sins. And if it had such great power in its types, if death shuddered so much at the figure, how would it not be in terror of the reality itself, pray tell? This blood is the salvation of our souls; by it the soul is cleansed; by it, beautified; by it, inflamed. It makes our intellect brighter than fire; it renders our soul more radiant than gold. This blood has been poured forth and opened the way to heaven.[42]

For what is the bread? The body of Christ. And what do they become who partake of it? The body of Christ: not many bodies, but one body. For as the bread consisting of many grains is made one, so that the grains nowhere appear; they exist indeed, but their difference is not seen by reason of their conjunction; so are we joined with each other and with Christ: there not being one body for you, and another for your neighbor to be nourished by, but the very same for all. Wherefore also he adds, "For we all partake of one bread." Now if we are all nourished of the same, why do we not also show forth the same love, and become also in this respect one?[43]

Let us not, I pray you, let us not slay ourselves by our irreverence, but with all awefulness and purity draw nigh to It; and when you see It set before you, say to yourself, "Because of this Body I am no longer earth and ashes, no longer a prisoner, but free: because of this I hope for heaven, and to receive the good things therein, immortal life, the portion of angels, converse with Christ; this body, nailed and scourged, was more than death could stand against; this body the very sun saw sacrificed, and turned aside his beams; for this both the veil was rent in that moment, and rocks were burst asunder, and all the earth was shaken. Thus even that body, the blood stained, the pierced, and that out of which gushed the saving fountains, the one of blood, the other of water, for all the world."[44]

Would you also learn of its power from another source? Ask of her diseased with an issue of blood, who laid hold not of Itself but of the garment with which It was clad; nay not of the whole of this, but of the hem: ask of the sea, which bore It on its back: ask even of the devil himself, and say, "Whence have you that incurable stroke? Whence have you no longer any power? Whence are you captive? By whom have you been seized in your flight?" And he will give you no other answer but this, "The body that was crucified." By this were his goads broken in pieces; by this was his head crushed; by this were the powers and the principalities made a show of.[45]

Let us draw nigh to him then with fervency and with inflamed love, that we may not have to endure punishment. For in proportion to the greatness of the benefits bestowed on us, so much the more exceedingly are we chastised when we show ourselves unworthy of the bountifulness. This body, even lying in a manger, the Magi reverenced. Indeed, men profane and barbarous, leaving their country and their home, both set out on a long journey, and when they came, with fear and great trembling worshipped him. Let us, then, at least imitate those barbarians, we who are citizens of heaven. For they indeed when they saw him but in a manger, and in a hut, and no such thing was in sight as you behold now, drew nigh with great awe; but you behold him not in the manger, but on the altar, not a woman holding him in her arms, but the priest standing by, and the Spirit with exceeding bounty hovering over the gifts set before us. You do not see merely this body itself as they did, but you know also Its power, and the whole economy, and are ignorant of none of the holy things which are brought to pass by It, having been exactly initiated into all.[46]

For this Table is the sinews of our soul, the bond of our mind, the foundation of our confidence, our hope, our salvation, out light, our life. When with this sacrifice we depart into the outer world, with much confidence we shall tread the sacred threshold, fenced round on every side with a kind of golden armor.[47]

Perceive how that which is more precious than all things is seen by you on earth; and not seen only, but also touched, but likewise eaten.[48]

SAINT CYRIL OF JERUSALEM
(Bishop of Jerusalem, 315–390?)

Then when the spiritual sacrifice, the bloodless act of worship is complete, we beseech God, on the ground of that sacrifice of propitiation, for the common peace of the churches; for the stability of the world; for kings; for our soldiers and allies; for the sick and afflicted; in fact, we pray for all who need help, for them we offer this sacrifice. Next we remember those who have fallen asleep before us; first the Patriarchs, Apostles, Martyrs; that by their prayers and intercessions God may receive our supplication. After that we pray for the holy Fathers and bishops who have already fallen asleep; and, in short, all of the departed, believing that it will be the greatest advantage for the souls of those for whom this supplication is offered when the holy and awful sacrifice is set before God.

We offer up Christ, sacrificed for our sins, propitiating our compassionate God on their behalf, and on our own.[49]

Therefore, when he has spoken and says about the bread, "This is my Body," who will have the nerve to doubt any longer? And when he affirms clearly, "This is my Blood," who will then doubt, saying that it is not his Blood?

Once, by his own will, he changed water into wine at Cana of Galilee; is he not worthy of belief when he changes wine into blood? . . .

Therefore do not consider them as bare bread and wine; for, according to the declaration of the Master, they are Body and Blood.[50]

SAINT HILARY OF POITIERS
(Bishop of Poitiers, 315)

If the Word has indeed become flesh, and we indeed receive the Word as flesh in the Lord's supper, how are we not to believe that he dwells in us by his nature, he who, when he was born a man, has assumed the nature of our flesh that is bound inseparably with himself, and has mingled the nature of his flesh to his eternal nature in the mystery of the flesh that was to be communicated to us?[51]

About the truth of his Flesh and Blood there is left no room for doubt. For by the Lord's own words and by our faith [we know] that it is truly flesh and truly blood. And when we have received and drunk these realities it comes about that we are in Christ and Christ is in us. Is this not the truth? Let it happen that those who deny that Christ is God deny this also. He is in us through his Flesh, and we are in him, and that by which we are with him is in God.[52]

''As the living Father has sent me and as I live through the Father, so he who shall eat my flesh shall live through me" (Jn 6:57). Consequently, he lives through the Father, and, as he lives through the Father, we live in the same manner through his flesh. Every illustration is adapted to the nature of our understanding in order that we may grasp the matter under discussion by means of the example that is set before us. Accordingly, this is the cause of our life, that we, who are carnal, have Christ dwelling in us through his flesh, and through him we shall live in that state in which he lives through the Father.[53]

SAINT GREGORY OF NAZIANZUS
(Bishop of Nazianzus, 330)

[Gregory's sister, Gorgonia, was desperately ill.] What remedy did she find for her suffering? Here is her secret. She despaired of any other relief, and had recourse to the Physician of all mankind. She waited till dead of night, during a slight alleviation of her condition, and fell on her knees before the altar with faith, calling with a loud cry and with every kind of invocation upon him who is honored upon the altar, recalling to him all his mighty acts, whenever they were performed (for she was well versed in the stories of the old and new dispensation). Then at last she ventured on an act of reverent and noble impudence, imitating the woman who staunched the flow of blood by means of the fringe of Christ's shawl (Mt 9:20). What did she do? She bowed her head over the altar, and with another loud cry, and with a wealth of tears, like the one who in times gone by bathed Christ's feet (Lk 7:38), and she threatened that she would not leave off until she was restored to health. Then she applied her whole body to this medicine which she had with her, namely so much of the antitypes of the precious body and blood as she had treasured in her hand, mingling it with her tears. And, wonder of wonders, she at once perceived that she was healed, and went away, light in body and soul and mind, having received what she had hoped for as a reward for that hope, and having gained strength of body because of her strength of soul. An extraordinary story, but quite true.[54]

I have recovered from my troublesome illness, and I hasten to write to you, as one responsible for my restored health.

For the tongue of a priest, speaking wisely of the Lord, arouses the sick to health. Now therefore do something even greater when you exercise the priestly office: release me from the great burdens of my sins, as you take hold of the resurrection sacrifice [Eucharist]. . . . Do not hesitate to pray for me, to be my ambassador, when by your word you draw down the Word, when with a stroke which draws no blood you sever the body and blood of the Lord, using your voice as your sword.[55]

SAINT GREGORY OF NYSSA
(Bishop of Nyssa, 335)

The God who was manifested mingled himself with the nature that was doomed to death, in order that by communion with the divinity, human nature may be deified together with him. It is for this purpose that by the divine plan of his grace he plants himself in believers by means of that flesh, composed of bread and wine, blending himself with the bodies of believers, so that man also may share in immortality by union with the immortal.[56]

SAINT AMBROSE
(Bishop of Milan, 339–397)

The sacrament which you receive is effected by the words of Christ. Now if the words of Elijah had the power to call down fire from heaven (1 Kings 18:38), will not the words of Christ have the power to change the character [species] of the elements? You have read, in the account of the creation of the universe: "He himself spoke, and they were made: he commanded, and they were created" (Ps 33:9). The words of Christ, then, could make out of nothing that which did not exist; can it not change things which do exist into what they are not? For to give things their original nature is more marvelous than to change their natures. But why do we use arguments? Let us make use of appropriate examples, and by the mysteries of the incarnation let us establish the truth of the mystery. When the Lord Jesus was born of Mary did that birth have the normal, natural antecedent? In the usual order of things, birth results from the union of man and woman. It is clear, then, that the Virgin gave birth outside of the order of nature. And this body which we bring about through consecration is from the Virgin. Why do you look for the order of nature here, in the case of the body of Christ, when the Lord Jesus himself was born of a virgin outside of the natural order? It was certainly the genuine flesh of Christ that was crucified, that was buried: then certainly the sacrament is the sacrament of that flesh. The Lord Jesus himself proclaims, "This is my body." Before the blessing of the heavenly words something of another character is spoken of; after consecration it is designated "body". He himself speaks of his blood. Before the consecration it is spoken of as something else; after the consecration it is spoken of as "blood". And you say, "Amen", that is, "It is true." What the mouth speaks, let the mind within confess; what the tongue utters, let the heart feel.[57]

We have seen the High Priest coming to us; we have seen and heard him offering his blood for us. We priests follow, as well as we can, so that we may offer sacrifice for the people. Though we claim no merit, we are to be honored in the sacrifice; for, although Christ is not now visibly offered, yet he is himself offered on earth when the body of Christ is offered. Moreover, it is made clear that he himself offers in us, since it is his words which sanctify the sacrifice which is offered.[58]

SAINT AUGUSTINE OF HIPPO
(Bishop of Hippo, 354)

Was that bread made of one grain of wheat? Were there not, rather, many grains? However, before they became bread these grains were separate; they joined together in water after a certain amount of crushing. For, unless the grain is ground and moistened with water, it cannot arrive at that form which is called bread.

So, too, you were previously ground, as it were, by the humiliation of your fasting and the sacrament of exorcism. Then came the baptism of water; you were moistened, as it were, so as to arrive at the form of bread. But, without fire, bread does not yet exist. What, then, does fire signify? The chrism. For the sacrament of the Holy Spirit is the oil of our fire.[59]

On the cross he accomplished a great deal: He has opened the treasure containing our ransom. When his side was pierced with the lance there trickled from it the ransom price of the whole world. The faithful and the martyrs have been purchased by his blood, but the faith of the martyrs is a faith which has proved itself: it is sealed in their own blood. They have paid back what they received, and have fulfilled the words of the evangelist John: "As Christ has laid down his life for us we ought to lay down our lives for the brethren" (1 Jn 3:16). And again we read: "When you sit down to dine with a ruler keep in mind who is before you" (Prov 23:1, 2).

The ruler's table is that on which the Lord himself is the food on the table. Nobody gives himself to his guests as food: But Christ the Lord does so. He is the host, the food and the drink. The martyrs have understood what they have eaten and drunk so that they might render a similar return.[60]

Christ, our Lord, has offered in suffering for us the flesh which he received from us at birth. He has become prince of priests forever and has left the disposition of sacrifice which you see, namely his own flesh and blood. The water and blood when issued from his body when struck by the lance has remitted our sins. Mindful of this grace that achieves your salvation which he, being God, operates in you, approach Communion with fear and trembling. Recognize in the bread what hangs on the Cross; recognize in the chalice the water and blood trickling from his side.

The old sacrifices of the people of God prefigured in a variety of ways this unique sacrifice to come. Christ is the sheep by reason of innocence and simplicity of soul; he is the goat through his resemblance to our sinful flesh. And whatever else the sacrifices of the Old Testament have foretold in many divine ways pertain to this one divine revelation of the New Testament.[61]

You are what you receive by the grace which redeemed you.[62]

Consider more carefully the manner in which bread is made. How is it done? First, there is the threshing, then it is ground, kneaded, baked; in the kneading it is refined, in baking it becomes solid. Where is your process of sifting? In fastings, in vigils, in exorcisms. Kneading is not done without water: you were baptized. Baking is troublesome but essential. How are you baked? In the fire of temptations which are an intimate part of life. But how is it essential? "The furnace proves the potter's vessels; so the trial of tribulation proves the just" [Sir 27:5].[63]

Just as individual grains unite in the kneading to form one bread, so the harmonious charity unites all into the one body of Christ. The grapes are to the blood of Christ what the grains of wheat are to his body. For the wine is formed by being pressed, and many individual drops unite in a single flow and become wine. Thus the mystery of unity is present in both the bread and the wine.[64]

The whole redeemed community, the congregation and fellowship of the saints, is offered as a universal sacrifice to God by the great Priest who offered himself in suffering for us in the form of a servant, that we might be the Body of so great a Head. This form of a servant he offered, in this he was offered; for in this he is mediator, priest, and sacrifice. So the Apostle exhorted us to "present our bodies as a living sacrifice" (Rom 12:1) . . . ; We ourselves are the whole sacrifice. . . . This is the sacrifice of Christians; the "many who are one body in Christ" (Rom 12:5). The sacrifice the Church celebrates in the sacrament of the altar, which the faithful know well, where it is shown to her that in this thing which she offers she herself is offered.[65]

Judas, to whom the Lord gave the piece of bread, gave the devil his chance to enter him (Jn 13:26), not by receiving something evil, but by receiving something in an evil way. So when a man receives the sacrament of the Lord unworthily the result is not that the sacrament is evil because he is evil, nor that he has received nothing at all because he has not received it for his salvation. It is just as much the Lord's body and blood when a man "eats and drinks judgment to himself" (1 Cor 11:29) by partaking unworthily.[66]

He took earth from earth, because flesh is from the earth, and he took Flesh of the flesh of Mary. He walked on earth in that same Flesh, and gave that same Flesh to us to be eaten for our salvation. Moreover no one eats that Flesh unless he has first adored it . . . and we sin by not adoring.[67]

Who is the Bread of heaven except Christ? But in order that men might eat the bread of angels, the Lord of the angels became a man. If this had not happened, we would not have his Flesh; if we did not have his Flesh, we would not eat the Bread of the altar.[68]

Not only do we become Christians; we become Christ. . . . If he is the Head and we are the members, then together we are the whole man.[69]

SAINT CYRIL OF ALEXANDRIA
(Bishop of Alexandria, 403)

It was necessary for him to be present in us in a divine manner through the Holy Spirit: to be mixed, as it were, with our bodies by means of his holy flesh and precious blood, for us to have him in reality as a sacramental gift which gives life, in the form of bread and wine. And so that we should not be struck down with horror, at seeing flesh and blood displayed on the holy tables of our churches, God adapts himself to our weakness and infuses the power of life into the oblations and changes them into the effective powers of his own flesh, so that we may have them for life-giving reception, and that the body of life may prove to be in us a life-giving seed.[70]

"He that eats my flesh," says he, "and drinks my blood abides in me and I in him." For as if one should join wax with other wax, he will surely see (I suppose) the one in the other; in a like manner (I deem) he who receives the flesh of our Savior Christ and drinks his precious blood, as he says, is found one with him, commingled as it were and intermingled with him through the participation, so that he is found in Christ, Christ again in him.[71]

SAINT FAUSTUS OF RIEZ
(Monk/Bishop, c. 495)

Since the body he assumed was to be taken away from our sight and returned to the stars, it was necessary that he should consecrate for us on this day the sacrament of his body and blood so that it might be legitimately worshipped continuously in this sacrament which he had offered once for our redemption. Since the redemption was in continuous and tireless motion for the redemption of men, the offering of the redemption should likewise be perpetual and the perennial victim be abiding in memory and be always present in our hearts.[72]

Away, then, with all the equivocation of the infidels, since the author of the gift is also the one who guarantees its truth. For a visible priest in virtue of a secret power converts by his own words visible elements into his body and blood saying, "Take and eat: this is my body," and continuing the consecration, "Drink of this: this is my blood" (Mt 26:26, 28). Accordingly, just as at the Lord's behest the lofty heavens, the depths of the sea and the expanses of the earth were suddenly created out of nothing, so by the same divine omnipotence in the spiritual words of the sacrament his power is revealed and reality obeys it.

Ask yourself, then, you who have been regenerated in Christ, how great and how celebrated are the achievements of the divine blessing, and do not judge it extraordinary or impossible that what is earthly and mortal should be changed into the very substance of Christ.

Long estranged from life and a stranger to divine mercy and the way of salvation, you were nothing but an exile because of the death of your soul. But suddenly introduced to the laws of God and renewed by the mysteries of salvation you passed, not visibly, but by faith, into the body of the Church.

By a hidden purification you deserved to be transformed from a son of perdition into an adopted son of God. Retaining all your physical dimensions you have visibly become greater than your former self without any quantitative increase, and while retaining your original personality you have become a very different person by the workings of faith. Nothing has been added to your stature externally, but you have undergone a complete interior transformation, as man has become the son of Christ and Christ has taken form in the soul of man. Just as without bodily perception you have been rid of your baseness and invested with a new dignity, just as Christ has healed your wounds, cleansed your stains, and washed your uncleanness, without any help from your eyes or your senses, so when you approach the holy altar to be nourished by the food from heaven, contemplate, adore and marvel at the sacred body and blood of your God, grasp it with your mind, take it to heart, and above all absorb it into your interior being.[73]

What wonder is it if he who by a word can create can also convert created objects by a mere word? Indeed it seems to be a lesser miracle to change for the better an already created object. What, pray, can be difficult to him who without difficulty formed man from the slime of the earth, who could clothe him in his own divine image, easily recall him from hell, restore him from perdition, raise him from the dust, elevate him from earth to heaven, make him into an angel, endow his human body with his own radiance, sublimate his shadow to share in his kingdom? Thus he who assumed our human body in all its frailty would assume us and invest us with his own immortality. For which glorious resurrection may he deign to prepare us by works of piety, who lives and reigns for ever and ever. Amen.[74]

SAINT CAESARIUS OF ARLES
(Bishop of Arles, 470–542)

And so, dearly beloved brethren, let us each examine his conscience, and when he sees that he has been wounded by some sin, let him first strive to cleanse his conscience by prayer, fasting, almsgiving, and so dare to approach the Eucharist. If he recognizes his guilt and is reluctant to approach the holy altar, he will be quickly pardoned by the divine mercy, "For whoever exalts himself will be humbled, and whoever humbles himself will be exalted" (Mt 23:12). If then, as I have said, a man, conscious of his sins, humbly decides to stay away from the altar until he reforms his life he will not be afraid of being completely excluded from the eternal banquet of heaven.

I ask you then, brethren, to pay careful attention. If no one dares approach an influential man's table in tattered, soiled garments, how much more should one refrain in reverence and humility from the banquet of the eternal king, that is, from the altar of the Lord, if one is smitten with poisonous envy, or anger, or is full of rage and fury? For it is written, "Go first and be reconciled to your brother, and then come and offer your gift" (Mt 5:24). And again, " 'Friend, how did you come in here without a wedding garment?' And when he kept silent the man said to the attendants, 'bind his hands and feet and cast him forth into the darkness outside where there will be weeping and gnashing of teeth'" (Mt 22:12-13). The same sentence awaits the man who dares present himself at the wedding feast, that is at the Lord's table, if he is guilty of drunkenness, or adultery, or retains hatred in his heart.[75]

SAINT JOHN OF DAMASCUS
(650-725)

If the Word of God is living and powerful, and if the Lord does all things whatsoever he wills; if he said, "Let there be light", and it happened; if he said, "Let there be a firmament", and it happened; . . . if finally the Word of God himself willingly became a man and made flesh for himself out of the most pure and undefiled blood of the holy and ever Virgin, why should he not be capable of making bread his Body and wine and water his Blood? . . . God said, "This is my Body", and, "This is my Blood."[76]

Let us partake of the Divine Coal . . . in order that we may be inflamed and divinized by our share in the divine fire. Isaiah saw [this] coal. Now coal is not simple wood but rather wood united with fire. So also the Bread of Communion is not simple bread but bread united with the Divinity.[77]

STEPHEN, BISHOP OF AUTUN
(1139)

O outstanding miracle! O marvelous and most divine Sacrament! . . . What the priest takes up is not what he replaces on the altar. That which is taken up and placed down seems to be the same in appearance, color, and taste. Completely different, however, is that which appears from that which lies hidden within. Common bread is lifted up from the altar; the immortal Flesh of Christ is set down upon it. What was natural food has become spiritual food. What was the momentary refreshment of man has been made the eternal and unfailing nourishment of angels.[78]

LATERAN COUNCIL IV
(1215)

There is one universal Church of the faithful, outside of which no one at all is saved. In this Church Jesus Christ is both priest and sacrifice. In the Sacrament of the Altar, under the species of bread and wine, His Body and Blood are truly contained, the bread having been transubstantiated into this Body and the wine into His Blood by the divine power. In order to complete the mystery of unity, we receive from Him what He received from us. And no one is able to confect this Sacrament except the priest who is properly ordained according to the keys of the Church, which Jesus Christ Himself gave to the Apostles and their successors.[79]

SAINT FRANCIS OF ASSISI
(1221)

We clerics cannot overlook the sinful neglect and ignorance some people are guilty of with regard to the holy Body and Blood of our Lord Jesus Christ. They are careless, too, about his holy name and the writings which contain his words, the words that consecrate his Body. We know his Body is not present unless the bread is first consecrated by these words. Indeed, in this world there is nothing of the most high himself that we can possess and contemplate with our eyes, except his Body and Blood. . . . Those who are in charge of the sacred mysteries, and especially those who are careless about their task, should realize that the chalices, corporals, and altar linens where the Body and Blood of our Lord Jesus Christ are offered in sacrifice should be completely suitable. And besides, many clerics reserve the Blessed Sacrament in unsuitable places or carry It about irreverently, or receive It unworthily, or give It to all-comers without distinction. . . . Surely, we cannot be left unmoved by loving sorrow for all this; in his love, God gives himself into our hands; we touch and receive him daily into our mouths. Have we forgotten that we must fall into his hands? And so we must correct these and other abuses. If the Body of our Lord Jesus Christ has been left abandoned somewhere contrary to all the laws, It should be removed and put in a place that is prepared properly for It, where It can be kept safe.[80]

Our whole being should be seized with fear, the whole world should tremble and heaven rejoice, when Christ the Son of the living God is present on the altar in the hands of the priest. What wonderful majesty! What stupendous condescension! O sublime humility! O humble sublimity! That the Lord of the whole universe, God and the Son of God, would humble himself like this and hide under the form of a little bread, for our salvation.[81]

SAINT CLARE OF ASSISI
(1194–1253)

I pray you, O gentle Jesus, having redeemed me by my baptism from original sin, so now by your precious Blood, which is offered and received throughout the world, deliver me from all evils, past, present, and to come.

By your most cruel death give me lively faith, a firm hope and perfect charity, so that I may love you with all my soul and strength. Make me firm and steadfast in good works and grant me perseverance in your service so that I may be able to please you always.[82]

SAINT THOMAS AQUINAS
(1227–1274)

There were sacraments, namely signs of a sacred thing, in the Old Law; for instance the paschal lamb and other legal sacraments. These, however, only signified Christ's grace, and did not cause it. Hence Saint Paul speaks of "weak and beggarly elements" (Gal 1:9), for they neither contained nor conferred grace. The sacraments of the New Law do both. In them Christ's power, says Augustine, secretly works salvation under the covering of things of sense. A sacrament of the New Law is the visible figure of invisible grace, bearing its likeness and serving as its cause. Thus the washing by baptismal water represents the interior cleans-

ing from sin which is caused in virtue of the sacrament
of baptism.[83]

The Church's seven sacraments have common and
proper features. Common to all is the giving of grace,
common to all their being made up of words and
things. Christ is their author; he is the Word made
flesh, and as his flesh was sanctified and given sanctifying virtue because of the Word united to it, so sacramental things are sanctified and have sanctifying virtue
because of the words uttered in them. A word, says
Augustine, comes to the elements, and they become
a sacrament. Hence those sanctifying words are called
the form of the sacraments, and the sanctifying elements the matter: for instance, the matter of Baptism
is water, the matter of Confirmation is chrism. Every
sacrament, too, requires a minister who confers it with
the intention of bestowing and doing what the Church
bestows and does. If any of these three be defective,
that is, if the due form of words be not used, or the
due matter, or if the minister does not intend to bring
about the sacrament, then no sacrament is celebrated.
Fault in the recipient can be an obstacle to the effect
of the sacrament, for instance, if he receives the sacrament for outward show without his heart being prepared: he receives the sacrament, but not its effect, that
is, the grace of the Holy Spirit, for "the Holy Spirit of
instruction shuns all pretense" (Wis 1:5). Conversely,
there are others who never take a sacrament and yet
receive its effect from their devotion or desire.[84]

To be led forth from the physical world in order to seize the spiritual world is our human destiny, and therefore these sacramental reliefs come in a sensible guise. . . . Instruments are adapted to their principal cause, and this, as regards human well-being, is the Word Incarnate. How fitting then that he should come through to men in bodily fashion, and that divine virtue should continue to work invisibly in them through visible appearances.[85]

What is there awkward about visible and bodily things ministering to spiritual health? Are they not instruments of God, who was made flesh for us and suffered in this world? An instrument's virtue is not its own, but is imparted by the principal cause which sets it to work. Hence, the sacraments do not act from the properties of their natural elements, but because they have been adopted by Christ to communicate his strength.[86]

Christ touched lepers, and they were cleansed; his human action was really instrumental in the cure. Likewise his human nature entered into the spiritual effects of divine power. He shed his blood, and we are purified: "He washed us from our sins in his own blood"; and again, "Being justified freely . . . through faith in his blood" (Rev 1:5; Rom 3:24). His manhood, therefore, is the instrumental cause of our righteousness. It was composed of spirit and matter; spiritually he comes to us through faith, and corporeally through the sacraments, that we may make his holiness our own.

The noblest sacrament, consequently, is that wherein his body is really present. The Eucharist crowns all the other sacraments; and though all are instruments of grace, and his life and death work through them all, it is there that the sacramental causality reaches its height. [87]

Here, Lord Jesus, art thou both shepherd and green pasture. [88]

Among the immeasurable benefits God's goodness has bestowed on Christian people is a priceless dignity: "For what nation is there so great, who hath gods nigh unto them, as our Lord our God is unto us?" [Dt 4:7] The only begotten Son of God, intending to make us "partakers of the divine nature" (2 Pet 1:4), took our nature on himself, becoming man that he might make men gods. Everything of ours he adopted and turned to our salvation. His body he offered to God the Father on the altar of the cross as a sacrifice that we might be reconciled; his blood he shed both as a price to redeem us from wretched bondage and as a cleansing from all sin. [89]

Nothing more marvelous, for there it comes to pass that the substance of bread and wine is changed into the body and blood of Christ. He is there, perfect God and perfect man, under the show of a morsel of bread and a sup of wine. He is eaten by his faithful, but not mangled. Nay, when this sacrament is broken, in each piece he remains entire. The appearance of bread and wine remain, but the Thing is not bread or wine.

Here is faith's opportunity, faith which takes what is unseen or disguised, and keeps the senses from misjudging about the wonted appearances.[90]

Nothing more health-giving, for in this Sacrament sins are purged away, strength renewed, and the mind fortified with generous spiritual gifts. Offered in the Church for the living and the dead, it is meant for all, and all gain its benefits. Nothing is better appointed, for the sweetness of this sacrament none can tell. There comfort is drawn from the well-head of the spirit; there is found the memorial of Christ's exceeding love for us in his sufferings. That he might bring his boundless love home to the hearts of his faithful did he found this sacrament, after he celebrated the Passover with his disciples, when the Last Supper was ending: "Jesus knowing that his hour was come that he should depart out of this world, unto the Father, having loved his own which were in the world, he loved them to the end" (1 Cor 11:26). This sacrament is the everlasting "showing forth of his death until he come again" (Jn 16:22); the embodied fulfillment of all the ancient types and figures; the mighty joy of them that sorrow until he shall come again.[91]

Christ's true body, born from the Virgin Mary, is contained in the sacrament of the altar. To profess the contrary is heresy, because it detracts from the truth of Scripture, which records our Lord's own words, "This is my body." Persuading arguments may be found for the doctrine. One is that Christ would not be so intimately united to us were we to share only in his power; how much better that he should give us his very self, not merely his effects, for the perfect joining of head and members. There are other advantages too: what a proof of friendship, that he should feed us on himself; what a lift to hope, that we should be offered such familiar intercourse; what a test for faith, which merits by believing beyond reason and against sense. There are many others as well which cannot be exhaustively dealt with now.[92]

That Christ's true body and blood are present in this sacrament can be perceived neither by sense nor by reason, but by faith alone, which rests on God's authority. On the text, "This is my body which is given for you," Cyril comments that we must not doubt that this is true, but must take our Savior's word on faith; he is truth, and does not lie.[93]

This doctrine first of all brings out the dignity of the New Law. The sacrifices of the Old Law figuratively contained the true sacrifice of Christ's passion: "the law having the shadow of good things to come, not the very image of the things" (Heb 10:1). Rightly the New Law should surpass the Old, and offer Christ, not only in sign and figure, but in very truth. Therefore this sacrament, in which Christ is really present, is the culmination of all other sacraments in which his power is shared.[94]

Secondly, the mystery matches Christ's charity, which caused him to assume human nature in order to save us. Aristotle notes that it is in the name of friendship that friends should live together. Christ promised to reward his friends with his bodily presence: "Whereso-ever the body is, there will the eagles be gathered together" (Mt 24:28). Even during our pilgrimage he does not absent himself, but through his veritable body and blood he joins us to himself: "He that eateth my flesh and drinketh my blood abideth in me, and I in him" (Jn 6:57). By such familiar intercourse is this sacrament the greatest pledge of charity and encouragement of hope.[95]

Thirdly, the mystery invites an act of complete faith, accepting both the humanity and divinity of Christ: "You believe in God, believe also in me" (Jn 14:2). Faith is of things unseen; Christ's Godhead was his, and in this sacrament so also his manhood.[96]

Two qualities are required in the recipient, love desiring to be conjoined to Christ, and fear reverencing the sacrament. The first bids us approach, the second holds us back. If anybody knows from experience that daily Communion increases fervor without decreasing reverence, then let him go every day. But if anybody finds that reverence is lessened and devotion not much increased, then let him sometimes abstain, so as to draw nigh afterward with better dispositions.

Each person should be left to his own judgment. This is Augustine's advice, who quotes the examples of Zacchaeus, who made haste and came down from the tree and received Christ with joy (Lk 14:6), and the centurion, who confessed, "Lord, I am not worthy that thou shouldst enter under my roof" (Mt 8:8). Both honored our Savior, though in different ways, and both found mercy.[97]

POPE URBAN IV
(1261–1264)

[A]t the institution of this Sacrament, he himself said to the Apostles: "Do this in memory of me": so that for us the special and outstanding memorial of the extraordinary love with which he loved us would be this lofty and venerable Sacrament; a memorial, I say, marvelous and stupendous, delectable, pleasant, most salutary, and priceless above all things—a memorial in which signs have been innovated and marvels altered; a memorial in which there is all delight and sweetness to the taste, and in which the very sweetness of the Lord is tasted; a memorial indeed in which we attain support for our life and our salvation. This is the memorial most sweet and salvific in which we gratefully recall the memory of our redemption, in which we are drawn from evil, strengthened in good, and secure an increase in virtues and graces, the memorial in which we attain the corporeal Presence of the Savior himself.

Other things whose memory we keep we embrace spiritually and mentally: we do not thereby obtain their real presence. However, in this sacramental commemoration of Christ, Jesus Christ is present with us in his proper substance, although under another form. As he was about to ascend into heaven, he said to the Apostles and their helpers, "I will be with you all days even unto the consummation of the world." He comforted them with the gracious promise that he would remain and would be with them even by his corporeal presence. O worthy and uninterrupted memory, in which we recall that our death is dead, that our destruction has perished, and that the fruit affixed to the tree of the Cross has made it a life-giving tree for us. This is the glorious commemoration that fills the souls of the faithful with saving joy and supplies tears of devotion with an infusion of gladness. We exult remembering our wondrous liberation, and, remembering the Lord's Passion by which we have been liberated, we can scarcely contain our tears. Therefore in this most holy commemoration there is present to us simultaneously the joy of sweetness and tears, because in it we rejoice while crying and we cry while rejoicing devoutly. Ours are joyful tears and tear-filled joy, for the heart, filled with a powerful joy, spills forth sweet tears. O the immensity of divine love, the excess of divine piety, the abundance of divine generosity! For the Lord has given us all the things that lie beneath our feet and has given us dominion over all creatures of the earth. He has ennobled and raised up the dignity of man above the ministries of the angelic spirits. For they are administrators destined to minister unto those who have inherited salvation. And since his munificence toward us was so great, still willing to demonstrate with particular liberality his exuberant love for us, he revealed himself to us. Then, transcending even the fullness of generosity, he gave himself as our food. O singular and admirable liberality, when the Giver comes as the gift and is himself completely given with the gift! What great—even prodigal—generosity when anyone gives himself. Therefore he gave himself as nourishment, so that, since man had fallen through death, he might be lifted to life through food. Man fell by means of the food of the death-giving tree; man is raised up by means of the food of the life-giving tree. On the former hung the food of death, on the latter the nourishment of life. Eating of the former earned a wound; the taste of this latter restored health. Eating wounded us, and eating healed us. See how the cure has come forth whence the wound arose, and life has come forth whence death entered in. Indeed about that eating it was said: "On whatever day you eat it, you shall die"; about this eating, he has spoken: "If anyone eats this bread, he shall live forever." This is the food that fully restores, truly nourishes, completely satisfies —not the body but the heart, not the flesh but the [soul], not the stomach but the mind. Therefore to man who needed spiritual nourishment the merciful Savior himself provided, by a holy ordinance, a food to feed the soul, a food that is more powerful and more noble than any food of this world. There is manifested a liberality worthy of him and a work of kindness suitable to him, and the eternal Word of God, which is spiritual food and refreshment to his creatures, became Flesh and gave himself as food to a spiritual creature of flesh and body, namely, mankind. Mankind has eaten the bread of angels. Thus the Savior says, "My Flesh is real food."[98]

SAINT CATHERINE OF SIENA
(1347–1380)

[God the Father speaking:] Dearest daughter, contemplate the marvelous state of the soul who receives this bread of life, this food of angels, as she ought. When she receives this sacrament she lives in me and I in her. Just as the fish is in the sea and the sea is in the fish, so am I in the soul and the soul in me, the sea of peace. Grace lives in such a soul because, having received this bread of life in grace, she lives in grace. When this appearance of bread has been consumed, I leave behind the imprint of my grace, just as the seal that is pressed into warm wax leaves its imprint when it is lifted off. Thus does the power of this sacrament remain there in the soul; that is, the warmth of my divine charity, the mercy of the Holy Spirit remains there. The light of my only-begotten Son's wisdom remains there, enlightening the mind's eye. [The soul] is left strong, sharing in my strength and power, which make her strong and powerful against her selfish sensuality and against the devil and the world.

So you see, the imprint remains once the seal is lifted off. In other words, once the material appearances of the bread have been consumed, this true Sun returns to his orbit. Not that he had ever left it, for he is united with me. But my deep charity gave him to you as food for your salvation and for your nourishment in this life where you are pilgrim travelers, so that you would have refreshment and not forget the blessing of the Blood. I in my divine providence gave you this food, my gentle Truth, to help you in your need.

See, then, how bound and obligated you are to love me in return, since I have loved you so much, and because I am supreme eternal Goodness, deserving to be loved by you.[99]

THOMAS À KEMPIS

(1380–1471)

The Great Reverence with Which We Should Receive Christ

THE DISCIPLE

THESE are all Your words, O Christ, eternal Truth, though they were not all spoken at one time nor written together in one place. And because they are Yours and true, I must accept them all with faith and gratitude. They are Yours and You have spoken them; they are mine also because You have spoken them for my salvation. Gladly I accept them from Your lips that they may be the more deeply impressed in my heart. Words of such tenderness, so full of sweetness and love, encourage me; but my sins frighten me and an unclean conscience thunders at me when approaching such great mysteries as these. The sweetness of Your words invites me, but the multitude of my vices oppresses me. You command me to approach You confidently if I wish to have part with You, and to receive the food of immortality if I desire to obtain life and glory everlasting.

"Come to me," You say, "all you that labor and are burdened, and I will refresh you" (Mt 11:28). Oh, how sweet and kind to the ear of the sinner is the word by which You, my Lord God, invite the poor and needy to receive Your most holy Body! Who am I, Lord, that I should presume to approach You? Behold, the heaven of heavens cannot contain You, and yet You say: "Come, all of you, to Me."

What means this most gracious honor and this friendly invitation? How shall I dare to come, I who am conscious of no good on which to presume? How shall I lead You into my house, I who have so often offended in Your most kindly sight? Angels and archangels revere You, the holy and the just fear You, and You say: "Come to Me: all of you!" If You, Lord, had not said it, who would have believed it to be true? And if You had not commanded, who would dare approach?

Behold, Noah, a just man, worked a hundred years building the ark that he and a few others might be saved; how, then, can I prepare myself in one hour to receive with reverence the Maker of the world?

Moses, Your great servant and special friend, made an ark of incorruptible wood which he covered with purest gold wherein to place the tables of Your law; shall I, a creature of corruption, dare so easily to receive You, the Maker of law and the Giver of life?

Solomon, the wisest of the kings of Israel, spent seven years building a magnificent temple in praise of

Your name, and celebrated its dedication with a feast of eight days. He offered a thousand victims in Your honor and solemnly bore the Ark of the Covenant with trumpeting and jubilation to the place prepared for it; and I, unhappy and poorest of men, how shall I lead You into my house, I who scarcely can spend a half-hour devoutly—would that I could spend even that as I ought!

O my God, how hard these men tried to please You! Alas, how little is all that I do! How short the time I spend in preparing for Communion! I am seldom wholly recollected, and very seldom, indeed, entirely free from distraction. Yet surely in the presence of Your life-giving Godhead no unbecoming thought should arise and no creature possess my heart, for I am about to receive as my guest, not an angel, but the very Lord of angels.

Very great, too, is the difference between the Ark of the Covenant with its treasures and Your most pure Body with its ineffable virtues, between these sacrifices of the law which were but figures of things to come and the true offering of Your Body which was the fulfillment of all ancient sacrifices. Why, then, do I not long more ardently for Your adorable presence? Why do I not prepare myself with greater care to receive Your sacred gifts, since those holy patriarchs and prophets of old, as well as kings and princes with all their people, have shown such affectionate devotion for the worship of God?

The most devout King David danced before the ark of God with all his strength as he recalled the benefits once bestowed upon his fathers. He made musical instruments of many kinds. He composed psalms and ordered them sung with joy. He himself often played upon the harp when moved by the grace of the Holy Ghost. He taught the people of Israel to praise God with all their hearts and to raise their voices every day to bless and glorify Him. If such great devotion flourished in those days and such ceremony in praise of God before the Ark of the Covenant, what great devotion ought not I and all Christian people now show in the presence of this Sacrament; what reverence in receiving the most excellent Body of Christ!

Many people travel far to honor the relics of the saints, marveling at their wonderful deeds and at the building of magnificent shrines. They gaze upon and kiss the sacred relics encased in silk and gold; and behold, You are here present before me on the altar, my God, Saint of saints, Creator of men, and Lord of angels!

Often in looking at such things, men are moved by curiosity, by the novelty of the unseen, and they bear away little fruit for the amendment of their lives, especially when they go from place to place lightly and without true contrition. But here in the Sacrament of the altar You are wholly present, my God, the man Christ Jesus, whence is obtained the full realization of eternal salvation, as often as You are worthily and devoutly received. To this, indeed, we are not drawn by levity, or curiosity, or sensuality, but by firm faith, devout hope, and sincere love.

O God, hidden Creator of the world, how wonderfully You deal with us! How sweetly and graciously You dispose of things with Your elect to whom You offer Yourself to be received in this Sacrament!

This, indeed, surpasses all understanding. This in a special manner attracts the hearts of the devout and inflames their love. Your truly faithful servants, who give their whole life to amendment, often receive in Holy Communion the great grace of devotion and love of virtue.

Oh, the wonderful and hidden grace of this Sacrament which only the faithful of Christ understand, which unbelievers and slaves of sin cannot experience! In it spiritual grace is conferred, lost virtue restored, and the beauty, marred by sin, repaired. At times, indeed, its grace is so great that, from the fullness of the devotion, not only the mind but also the frail body feels filled with greater strength.

Nevertheless, our neglect and coldness is much to be deplored and pitied, when we are not moved to receive with greater fervor Christ in Whom is the hope and merit of all who will be saved. He is our sanctification and redemption. He is our consolation in this life and the eternal joy of the blessed in heaven. This being true, it is lamentable that many pay so little heed to the salutary Mystery which fills the heavens with joy and maintains the whole universe in being.

Oh, the blindness and the hardness of the heart of man that does not show more regard for so wonderful a gift, but rather falls into carelessness from its daily use! If this most holy Sacrament were celebrated in only one place and consecrated by only one priest in the whole world, with what great desire, do you think, would men be attracted to that place, to that priest of God, in order to witness the celebration of the divine Mysteries! But now there are many priests and Mass is offered in many places, that God's grace and love for men may appear the more clearly as the Sacred Communion is spread more widely through the world.

Thanks be to You, Jesus, everlasting Good Shepherd, Who have seen fit to feed us poor exiled people with Your precious Body and Blood, and to invite us with words from Your own lips to partake of these sacred Mysteries: "Come to Me, all you who labor and are burdened, and I will refresh you" (Mt 11:28).[100]

THE COUNCIL OF TRENT
(1562)

[Christ], our Lord and God, was once and for all to offer himself to God the Father by his death on the altar of the cross, to accomplish there an everlasting redemption. But because his priesthood was not to end with his death, at the Last Supper "on the night that he was betrayed," [he wanted] to leave his beloved spouse the Church a visible sacrifice (as the nature of man demands) by which the bloody sacrifice which he was to accomplish once and for all on the cross would be re-presented, its memory perpetuated until the end of the world, and its salutary power be applied to the forgiveness of the sins we daily commit.

The victim is one and the same: the same now offers through the ministry of priests, who then offered himself on the cross; only the manner of the offering is different. [101]

In this divine sacrifice which is celebrated in the Mass, the same Christ who offered himself once in a bloody manner on the altar of the cross is contained and offered in an unbloody manner. [102]

[In the Most Blessed Sacrament of the Eucharist] the body and blood, together with the whole soul and divinity, of our Lord Jesus Christ and, therefore, the whole Christ is truly, really, and substantially contained. [103]

Because Christ our Redeemer said that it was truly his body that he was offering under the species of bread, it has always been the conviction of the Church of God, and this holy Council now declares again, that by the consecration of the bread and wine there takes place a change of the whole substance of the bread into the substance of the body of Christ our Lord and of the whole substance of the wine into the substance of his blood. This change the Holy Catholic Church has fittingly and properly called transubstantiation. [104]

If it is unbecoming for anyone to approach any of the sacred functions except in a spirit of piety, assuredly, the more the holiness and divinity of this heavenly sacrament are understood by a Christian, the more diligently ought he to give heed lest he receive it without great reverence and holiness, especially when we read these terrifying words of the Apostle, "He that eateth and drinketh unworthily, eateth and drinketh judgment to himself, not discerning the body of the Lord." [105]

Finally, the holy council with paternal affection admonishes, exhorts, prays and beseeches through the bowels of the mercy of our God, that each and all who bear the Christian name will now at last agree and be of one mind in this sign of unity, in this bond of charity, in this symbol of concord, and that, mindful of so great a majesty and such boundless love of our Lord Jesus Christ, who gave his own beloved soul as the price of our salvation and his own flesh to eat, that they may believe and venerate these sacred mysteries of his body and blood with such constancy and firmness of faith, with such devotion of mind, with such piety and worship, that they may be able to receive frequently that supersubstantial bread and that it may truly be to them the life of the soul and the perpetual health of their mind, that being invigorated by its strength, they may be able after the journey of this miserable pilgrimage to arrive in their heavenly country, there to eat, without any veil, the same bread of angels which they now eat under sacred veils. [106]

SAINT TERESA OF JESUS
(1515–1582)

There must be someone . . . who will speak for [the neglect in the Blessed Sacrament of] Thy Son, for He has never defended Himself. Let this be the task for us, daughters, though, having regard to what we are, it is presumptuous of us to undertake it. Let us rely, however, on Our Lord's command to us to pray to Him, and, in fulfillment of our obedience to Him, let us beseech His Majesty, in the name of the good Jesus, that, as He has left nothing undone that He could do for us in granting sinners so great a favour, He may be pleased of His mercy to prevent Him from being so ill-treated. Since His Holy Son has given us this excellent way in which we can offer Him up frequently as a sacrifice, let us make use of this precious gift so that it may stay the advance of such terrible evil and irreverence as in many places is paid to this Most Holy Sacrament.[107]

If we pay no heed to Him save when we have received Him, and go away from Him in search of other and baser things, what can He do? Will He have to drag us by force to look at Him *and be with Him* because He desires to reveal Himself to us? No; for when He revealed Himself to all men plainly, and told them clearly who He was, they did not treat Him at all well—very few of them, indeed, even believed Him. So He grants us an exceeding great favour when He is pleased to show us that it is He Who is in the Most Holy Sacrament. But He will not reveal Himself openly and communicate His glories and bestow His treasures save on those whom He knows greatly desire Him, for these are His true friends. I assure you that anyone who is not a true friend and does not come to receive Him as such, after doing all in his power to prepare for Him, must never importune Him to reveal Himself to him. Hardly is the hour over which such a person has spent in fulfilling the Church's commandment than he goes home and tries to drive Christ out of the house. What with all his other business and occupations and worldly hindrances, he seems to be making all possible haste to prevent the Lord from taking possession of the house which is His own. [108]

SAINT ROBERT BELLARMINE
(1542–1621)

The Eucharistic Consecration pertains to the essence of sacrifice. . . . In the Eucharistic Consecration there occur three things in which the real definition of a true sacrifice is found. First, something profane [the bread and wine] becomes sacred. Bread, an earthly and common thing, is changed, by the Consecration, into the Body of Christ, the Most Holy of all things. Second, in the Consecration this sacred thing, which has been effected from the profane, is offered to God when it is placed on the altar. To place a victim on the altar is really to offer it to God, and, by the power of Con-

secration, it comes about that the Body and Blood of
Christ begin to be on the altar through the medium of
the priest's hands. . . . Third, through the Consecration, the things that are offered are ordained toward a
true, real, and eternal change and destruction, which
destruction is required by the definition of sacrifice.
Through the Consecration the Body of Christ takes
on the form of food, and of food to be eaten, and so
is ordained to change and destruction.[109]

SAINT MARGARET MARY
(1647–1690)

Oh, how fortunate you shall be to be able to receive
every day this divine Sacrament, to hold this God of
Love in your hands and place Him in your own heart! I
desire but this one grace, and long to be consumed like
a burning candle in His holy Presence every moment
of the life that remains to me. For that I would be willing, I think, to suffer all the pains imaginable till judgment day, if only I should not have to leave His sacred
presence. My only motive would be to be consumed
in honoring Him and to acknowledge the burning love
He shows us in this wonderful Sacrament. Here His
love holds Him captive till the end of time. It is of this
one can truly say, "Love triumphs, love enjoys / Love
finds in God its joys!"[110]

Life is such a heavy cross for me that I have no consolation but that of seeing the Heart of my adorable Savior

reign. He gives me the pleasure of suffering something whenever [the Devotion to the Sacred Heart] makes some new advance. But there is nothing I would not be willing to suffer for that. Even the most bitter sufferings are sweet in this adorable Heart, where everything is changed to love. I would like to be able to avenge on myself all the injuries done to my Savior Jesus Christ in the Blessed Sacrament.[111]

SAINT LOUIS DE MONTFORT
(1673–1716)

True Devotion to the Blessed Virgin at Holy Communion

BEFORE HOLY COMMUNION:

1. Place yourself humbly in the presence of God.

2. Renounce your corrupt nature and dispositions, no matter how good self-love makes them appear to you.

3. Renew your consecration [to Mary] saying, "I belong entirely to you, dear Mother, and all that I have is yours."

4. Implore Mary to lend you her heart so that you may receive her Son with her dispositions. Remind her that her Son's glory requires that he should not come into a heart so sullied and fickle as your own, which could not fail to diminish his glory and might cause him to leave. Tell her that if she will take up her abode in you to receive her Son—which she can do because

of the sovereignty she has over all hearts—he will be received by her in a perfect manner without danger of being affronted or being forced to depart. "God is in the midst of her. She shall not be moved" (Ps 45:6).

Tell her with confidence that all you have given her of your possessions is little enough to honor her, but that in Holy Communion you wish to give her the same gift as the Eternal Father gave her. Thus she will feel more honored than if you gave her all the wealth in the world. Tell her, finally, that Jesus, whose love for her is unique, still wishes to take his delight and repose in her even in your soul, even though it is poorer and less clean than the stable which he readily entered because she was there. Beg her to lend you her heart, saying, "O Mary, I take you for my all; give me your heart."

At Holy Communion:

After the Our Father, when you are about to receive our Lord, say to him three times the prayer, "Lord, I am not worthy." Say it the first time as if you were telling the Eternal Father that because of your evil thoughts and your ingratitude to such a good Father, you are unworthy to receive his only-begotten Son, but that here is Mary, his handmaid, who acts for you and whose presence gives you a special confidence and hope in him.

Say to God the Son, "Lord, I am not worthy", meaning that you are not worthy to receive him because of your useless and evil words and your carelessness in his service, but nevertheless you ask him to have pity on you because you are going to usher him into the house of his Mother and yours, and you will not let him go until he has made it his home. Implore him to rise and come to the place of his repose and the ark of his sanctification. Tell him that you have no faith in your own merits, strength and preparedness, like Esau, but only in Mary, your Mother, just as Jacob had trust only in Rebecca his mother. Tell him that although you are a great sinner you still presume to approach him, supported by his holy Mother and adorned with her merits and virtues.

Say to the Holy Spirit, "Lord, I am not worthy." Tell him that you are not worthy to receive the masterpiece of his love because of your lukewarmness, wickedness, and resistance to his inspirations. But, nonetheless, you put all your confidence in Mary, his faithful Spouse, and you say with Saint Bernard, "She is my greatest safeguard, the whole foundation of my hope." Beg him to overshadow Mary, his inseparable Spouse, once again. Her womb is as pure and her heart is as ardent as ever. Tell him that if he does not enter your soul neither Jesus nor Mary will be formed there nor will it be a worthy dwelling for them.

AFTER HOLY COMMUNION:

After Holy Communion, close your eyes and recollect yourself. Then usher Jesus into the heart of Mary; you are giving him to his Mother who will receive him with great love and give him the place of honor, adore him profoundly, show him perfect love, embrace him intimately in spirit and in truth, and perform many offices for him of which we, in our ignorance, would know nothing.

Or, maintain a profoundly humble heart in the presence of Jesus dwelling in Mary. Or be in attendance like a slave at the gate of his royal palace, where the King is speaking with the Queen. While they are talking with each other, with no need of you, go in spirit to heaven and to the whole world, and call upon all creatures to thank, adore, and love Jesus and Mary for you. "Come let us adore" (Ps 94:6).

Or, ask Jesus living in Mary that his kingdom may come upon earth through his holy Mother. Ask for divine wisdom, divine love, the forgiveness of your sins, or any other grace, but always through Mary and in Mary. Cast a look of reproach upon yourself and say, "Lord, do not look at my sins, let your eyes see nothing in me but the virtues and merits of Mary." Remembering your sins, you may add, "I am my own worst enemy and I am guilty of all these sins." Or, "Deliver me from the unjust and deceitful man" (Ps 42:1). Or again, "Dear Jesus, you must increase in my soul and I must decrease" (cf. Jn 3:30). "Mary, you must increase in me and I must always go on decreasing." "O Jesus and Mary, increase in me and increase in others around me."

There are innumerable other thoughts with which the Holy Spirit will inspire you, which he will make yours if you are thoroughly recollected and mortified, and constantly faithful to the great and sublime devotion which I have been teaching you. But remember, the more you let Mary act in your Communion, the more Jesus will be glorified. The more you humble yourself and listen to Jesus and Mary in peace and silence—with no desire to see, taste, or feel—then the more freedom you will give to Mary to act in Jesus' name and the more Jesus will act in Mary. For the just man lives everywhere by faith (Heb 10:38), but especially in Holy Communion, which is an action of faith.[112]

SAINT ALPHONSUS LIGUORI
(1696–1787)

An Act of Humility

Then, my soul, thou art even now about to feed on the most sacred flesh of Jesus! And art thou worthy? My God, and who am I, and who art Thou? I indeed know and confess who Thou art that givest Thyself to me; but dost Thou know who I am who am about to receive Thee? And is it possible, O my Jesus, that Thou who art infinite purity desirest to come and reside in this soul of mine, which has been so many times the dwelling of Thy enemy, and soiled with so many sins? I know, O my God, Thy great Majesty and my misery; I am ashamed to appear before Thee. Reverence would induce me to keep at a distance from Thee; but if I depart from Thee, O my life, whither shall I go? to whom shall I have recourse? and what will become of me? No, never will I depart from Thee; nay, even will I draw nearer and nearer to Thee. Thou art satisfied that I should receive Thee as food, Thou even invitest me to this. I come then, O my amiable Savior, I come to receive Thee this morning, all humbled and confused at the sight of my defects; but full of confidence in Thy tender mercy, and in the love which Thou bearest me.[113]

"The voice of my Beloved knocking: Open to Me, My sister, My love, My dove, My undefiled" (Song 5:2).

Such are the words which Jesus in the Blessed Sacrament speaks to those who love and desire him. Open to me, he says, O soul, thy heart, and there I will come to unite myself to thee; so that, being one with me, thou mayst become my sister by resemblance, my friend by participation in my riches, my dove by the gift of simplicity, my undefiled by the gift of purity, which I shall communicate to thee. And then he goes on to say, "Open to me, for my head is full of dew and my locks the drops of the night." As if he said: Consider, my beloved, that I have waited for thee all the night of the bad life thou hast led in the midst of darkness and error. Behold, now, instead of bringing scourges to chastise thee, I come in the Blessed Sacrament, with my hair full of heavenly dew, to extinguish in thee all impure desires towards creatures, and to kindle in thee the happy fire of my love. Come, then, O my beloved Jesus, and work in me what Thou wilt.[114]

Be assured that the time you spend with devotion before this most divine Sacrament will be the most profitable to you in life, and the source of your greatest consolation in death and in eternity. You must also be aware, that in a quarter of an hour's prayer spent in the presence of the Blessed Sacrament, you will perhaps gain more than in all the other spiritual exercises of the day.[115]

Jesus Christ finds means to console a soul that remains with a recollected spirit before the Most Blessed Sacrament, far beyond what the world can do with all its feasts and pastimes. Oh, how sweet a joy it is to remain with faith and tender devotion before an altar, and converse familiarly with Jesus Christ, who is there for the express purpose of listening to and graciously hearing those who pray to him; to ask his pardon for the displeasures which we have caused him; to represent our wants to him, as a friend does to a friend in whom he places all his confidence; to ask him for his graces, for his love, and for his kingdom; but above all, oh, what a heaven it is there to remain making acts of love towards that Lord who is on the very altar praying to the Eternal Father for us, and is there burning with love for us. Indeed that love it is which detains him there, thus hidden and unknown, and where he is even despised by ungrateful souls! But why should we say more? "Taste and see."[116]

To converse with Thee, O King of glory, no third person is needed; Thou art always ready in the Sacrament of the Altar to give audience to all. All who desire Thee always find Thee there, and converse with Thee face to face. And even if anyone at length succeeds speaking with a king, how many difficulties has he had to overcome before he can do so! Kings grant audiences only a few times a year; but Thou, in this Sacrament, grantest audience to all night and day, and whenever we please.[117]

SAINT JOHN VIANNEY
(1786–1859)

What does Jesus Christ do in the Eucharist? It is God who, as our Savior, offers himself each day for us to his Father's justice. If you are in difficulties and sorrows, he will comfort and relieve you. If you are sick, he will either cure you or give you strength to suffer so as to merit Heaven. If the devil, the world, and the flesh are making war upon you, he will give you the weapons with which to fight, to resist, and to win the victory. If you are poor, he will enrich you with all sorts of riches for time and for eternity. Let us open the door of his sacred and adorable Heart, and be wrapped about for an instant by the flames of his love, and we shall see what a God who loves us can do. O my God, who shall be able to comprehend?[118]

In times of discouragement when, after the consecration, I hold in my hands the most holy Body of our Lord, seeing myself to be only worthy of all hell, I say to myself: "Ah, if only I could take him with me! Hell would be sweet near him: it would not be painful to stay there suffering for all eternity if we were there together. . . . But then there would not be any more hell: the flames of love would extinguish those of justice.[119]

How great was the charity of Jesus Christ in choosing for the institution of the Eucharist the eve of the day he was to be put to death! At that moment all Jerusalem is on fire, all the populace enraged, all are plotting his ruin, and it is precisely at that moment that he is preparing for them the most unutterable pledge of his love. Men are weaving the blackest plots against him, and he is only occupied in giving them the most precious gift he has. They are only thinking of setting up an infamous cross for him that they may put him to death, and he is only thinking of setting up an altar that he may immolate himself every day for us. They are preparing to shed his Blood, and Jesus Christ wills that this same Blood shall be to us a draught of immortality for the consolation and happiness of our souls. Yes, we may say that Jesus Christ has loved us even to exhausting the riches of his love.[120]

Do not say that you are sinners, that you are too wretched, and that is why you dare not approach [the Eucharist]. You might just as well say that you are too ill, and that is why you will not try any remedy nor send for the doctor.[121]

By Communion, indeed, Jesus makes us all his own body, and identifies us with himself as the body with the head. He is not content with showing himself to us. He puts himself into our hands, into our mouth, mingling his substance with our substance, that we may become one spirit with him.[122]

When Jesus entered the house of Saint Elizabeth, although he was imprisoned in Mary's womb, he sanctified both mother and child; and Elizabeth exclaimed, "Whence comes so great a happiness to me, that the Mother of my God deigns to come to me?" I leave you to consider how much greater is the happiness of him who receives Jesus Christ in Holy Communion, not like Elizabeth, into his house, but into the depths of his heart, to be its protecting master, not six months, as in Elizabeth's case, but all through life.[123]

Why was Lazarus raised from the dead? Because he had often received our Lord into his house. The Savior loved him so much that he shed tears at seeing him lifeless. How then should he leave in the humiliation of the tomb those whom he has honored by his visit in Holy Communion, and who have eagerly desired him, and received him into a heart afire with love and clothed in purity?[124]

What a happiness was the aged Simeon's when he was pressing to his love-laden heart the child Jesus, who was enkindling and consuming that heart! "Now, Lord, let me die," he cried out. . . . Truly he was in ecstasy.

But we, are we not happier than Simeon? He could keep Jesus only for an instant; we can keep him always, if we will. He comes not only into our arms, but into our heart.[125]

O my God, what joy for a Christian who has faith! On rising from the holy table he goes away with all heaven in his heart.[126]

When we cannot come to church, let us turn at least in the direction of the tabernacle. The good God has no walls to stop him. Let us say five Our Fathers and Hail Marys as a spiritual communion. . . . We can receive the good God only once a day; but a soul on fire with love makes up for that by the desire of receiving him at every moment.[127]

When you go to Holy Communion you must always have an intention, and say, when you are on the point of receiving our Lord's Body: "O my good Father, who art in heaven, I offer thee, at this moment, thy dear Son, as he was taken down from the Cross and laid in the arms of the blessed Virgin, and offered by her to thee as a sacrifice for us. I offer him to thee by the hands of Mary to obtain such and such a grace: faith, charity, humility. . . ." My children, mark this well: whenever I obtained a grace, I asked it in this way, and it has never failed.[128]

If we really loved the good God, we should make it our joy and happiness to come and spend a few moments before the tabernacle to adore him, and ask him for the grace of forgiveness; and we should regard those moments as the happiest in our lives. Oh! how sweet and consoling are moments spent with the God of goodness. Are you in sorrow? Come cast yourself at his feet and you will feel quite consoled. Are you despised by the world? Come here and you will find a good friend whose faithfulness will never fail you. Are you tempted? It is here that you will find strong and terrible weapons to vanquish your enemies. Do you fear the formidable judgment which has made the greatest saints tremble? Profit by the time in which your God is the God of mercies, and while it is so easy to win your pardon from him. Are you oppressed by poverty? Come here and you will find a God infinitely rich, and who will tell you that his wealth is yours, not in this world, but in the next. . . . Sinners, ask him with tears and sorrow for the pardon of your sins, and you are sure to obtain it. You who are reconciled with him, beg for the precious gift of perseverance. Oh! Tell him that if you are to offend him again, you would far rather die. Would you begin to taste the joy of the saints? Come here and you will know the happy beginnings of it.[129]

We ought to visit him often. How dear to him is a quarter of an hour spared from our occupations or from some useless employment, to come and pray to him, visit him, and console him for all the ingratitude he receives! When he sees pure souls hurrying to him, he smiles at them. They come with that simplicity which pleases him so much, to ask pardon for all sinners, and for the insults of so many who are ungrateful. [130]

SAINT PETER JULIAN EYMARD
(1811–1868)

In the Eucharist, Jesus exposes Himself without protection to the insults and outrages of the impious; and the number of His new executioners is very great.

His goodness is disregarded and despised by a large number of bad Christians. His holiness is defiled by so many profanations and sacrileges, and that by His own children and His best friends. [131]

The Eucharist is not only the end but the continuation of the Incarnation and Passion of the Savior. Under the form of the Sacrament, Jesus continues the poverty of His birth, the obedience of Nazareth, the humility of His life, the humiliation of His Passion, His state of Victim on the Cross. [132]

The Eucharist, behold the Christian's treasure, his delight on earth. Since Jesus is in the Eucharist for him personally, his whole life ought to be drawn to it like a magnet to its center. [133]

With the Divine Host, the adorer fares well everywhere. As far as he is concerned, there is no exile or desert or privation or misfortune; he has everything in the adorable Eucharist. All one need do to punish him, render him unhappy, or make him die of sadness, is to take the God of the Tabernacle away from him. Life would then be for him but a prolonged agony, and all the goods and glories of this world but woeful chains. Like the captive Israelite, weeping on the shores of the river of Babylon at the thought of his beloved Jerusalem, the disciple of the Eucharist would not cease shedding bitter tears at the remembrance of the Cenacle.[134]

Nothing can compare with the ardor and power of a soul as it seeks its Beloved and longs for Him; it finds its happiness in longing for Him and seeking Him. The God of the Eucharist conceals Himself in order to be desired, veils Himself in order to become an object of contemplation; He wraps Himself in mystery in order to spur on and perfect the soul's love. The Holy Eucharist thus becomes a food ever new, ever powerful over the heart it inflames. Something akin to what happens in heaven then takes place: a hunger and thirst for God ever keen and ever satisfied; the loving soul penetrates the depths of divine love and never ceases discovering new riches therein; Jesus manifests Himself by degrees to the soul to draw it ever more purely and strongly to Himself.[135]

If the Christians continue to desert Jesus Christ in His temple, will not the Heavenly Father take away from them His well-beloved Son Whom they neglect?[136]

The adoration of Jesus in the Most Blessed Sacrament is the end of the Church Militant, just as adoration of God in His glory is the end of the Church Triumphant. A holy rivalry, a concert of prayer, a harmony of divine service should exist between the heavenly court and the Eucharistic court here below, between the adorer and his mother the Church. [137]

But as Jesus, the adorable Host, can no longer suffer or die, He needs a substitute victim that completes Him, that suffers in His place, and to that purpose He unites Himself with the penitent soul. Jesus will always be the ransom price of infinite value, and the faithful soul will, by its actual suffering, complete this new Calvary. This atoning soul weeps over the ingratitude of men, their crimes against the God of the Eucharist, Who is ignored, despised, and outraged by the majority of men and even by the closest and most honored friends of His Heart. It weeps over its own sins, which must be particularly displeasing to a Savior from Whom it receives only goodness and love. [138]

JOHN HENRY CARDINAL NEWMAN
(1801–1890)

It [the Mass] is not a mere form of words—it is a great action, the greatest action that can be on earth. It is, not the invocation merely, but, if I dare use the word, the evocation of the Eternal. He becomes present on the altar in flesh and blood, before whom angels bow and devils tremble. This is that awful event which is the end, and is the interpretation, of every part of the solemnity. Words are necessary, but as means, not as ends; they are not mere addresses to the throne of grace, they are instruments of what is far higher, of consecration, of sacrifice.[139]

Above all, let us pray Him to draw us to Him, and to give us faith. When we feel that His mysteries are too severe for us, and occasion us to doubt, let us earnestly wait on Him for the gift of humility and love. Those who love and are humble will apprehend them; —carnal minds do not seek them, and proud minds are offended at them;—but while love desires them, humility sustains them. . . . Let us pray Him to give us an earnest longing after Him—a thirst for His presence—an anxiety to find Him—a joy on hearing that He is to be found, even now, under the veil of sensible things,—and a good hope that *we* shall find Him there. Blessed indeed are they that have not seen, and yet have believed.[140]

In truth, our Merciful Saviour has done much more for us than reveal the wonderful doctrines of the Gospel; He has enabled us to apply them. . . . But how should we bring home His grace to ourselves? . . . How secure the comfortable assurance that He loves us personally, and will change our hearts, which we feel to be so earthly, and wash away our sins, which we confess to be so manifold, unless He had given us Sacraments —means and pledges of grace—keys which open the treasure-house of mercy.[141]

To believe, and not to revere, to worship familiarly, and at one's ease, is an anomaly and a prodigy unknown even to false religions, to say nothing of the true one. . . . Worship, forms of worship—such as bowing the knee, taking off the shoes, keeping silence, a prescribed dress, and the like—are considered as necessary for a due approach to God.[142]

The Benediction of the Blessed Sacrament is one of the simplest rites of the Church. . . . It is our Lord's solemn benediction of His people, as when He lifted up His hands over the children, or when He blessed His chosen ones when He ascended up from Mount Olivet. As sons might come before a parent before going to bed at night. So, . . . the great Catholic family comes before the Eternal Father, after the bustle or toil of the day, and He smiles upon them, and sheds upon them the light of His countenance. It is a full accomplishment of what the Priest invoked upon the Israelites, "The Lord bless thee and keep thee; the Lord show His face to thee and have mercy on thee; the Lord turn His countenance to thee and give thee peace."[143]

POPE LEO XIII
(1878–1903)

The Eucharist, according to the testimony of the holy Fathers, should be regarded as in a manner a continuation and extension of the Incarnation. For in and by it the substance of the incarnate Word is united with individual men, and the supreme Sacrifice offered on Calvary is in a wondrous manner renewed, as was signified beforehand by Malachy in the words: "In every place there is sacrifice, and there is offered to My name a pure oblation" (Mal 1:2). And this miracle, itself the very greatest of its kind, is accompanied by innumerable other miracles; for here all the laws of nature are suspended; the whole substance of the bread and wine are changed into the Body and the Blood; the species of bread and wine are sustained by the divine power without the support of any underlying substance.[144]

In a word this Sacrament is, as it were, the very soul of the Church; and to it the grace of the priesthood is ordered and directed in all its fulness and in each of its successive grades. From the same source the Church draws and has all her strength, all her glory, her every supernatural endowment and adornment, every good thing that is here.[145]

BLESSED FAUSTINA KOWALSKA
(1905–1938)

When I was in church waiting for confession, I saw the same rays (that is, as those depicted on the revealed image of the Divine Mercy) issuing from the monstrance and they spread throughout the church. This lasted all through the service. After the benediction (the rays came forth) on both sides and returned again to the monstrance. Their appearance was bright and clear as crystal. I asked Jesus that He deign to light the fire of His love in all souls that were cold. Beneath these rays a heart will be warmed even if it were like a block of ice; even if it were as hard as rock, it will crumble into dust.[146]

Once, when my confessor [Father Sopocko] was saying Mass, I saw, as usual, the Child Jesus on the altar, from the time of the Offertory. However, a moment before the Elevation, the priest vanished from my sight, and Jesus alone remained. When the moment of the Elevation approached, Jesus took the Host and the Chalice in His little hands and raised them together, looking up to heaven, and a moment later I saw my confessor again. I asked the Child Jesus where the priest had been during the time I had not seen him. Jesus answered, "In My Heart." But I could not understand anything more of these words of Jesus.[147]

Oh what awesome mysteries take place during Mass! A great mystery is accomplished in the Holy Mass. With great devotion we should listen to and take part in this death of Jesus. One day we will know what God is doing for us in each Mass, and what sort of gift He is preparing in it for us. Only His divine love could permit that such a gift be provided for us. O Jesus, my Jesus, with what great pain is my soul pierced when I see this fountain of life gushing forth with such sweetness and power for each soul, while at the same time I see souls withering away and drying up through their own fault. O Jesus, grant that the power of mercy embrace these souls.[148]

After Communion today, Jesus told me how much He desires to come to human hearts. "I desire to unite Myself with human souls; My great delight is to unite Myself with souls. Know, My daughter, that when I come to a human heart in Holy Communion, My hands are full of all sorts of graces which I want to give to the soul. But souls do not even pay attention to Me; they leave Me to Myself and busy themselves with other things. Oh, how sad I am that souls do not recognize Love! They treat me as a dead object." [149]

I remind you, My daughter, that as often as you hear the clock strike the third hour in the afternoon, immerse yourself completely in My mercy, adoring and glorifying it; invoke its omnipotence for the whole world, and particularly for poor sinners. . . . My daughter, try your best to make the Stations of the Cross in this hour, provided that your duties permit it; and if you are not able to make the Stations of the Cross, then at least step into the chapel for a moment and adore the Most Blessed Sacrament, My Heart, which is full of mercy. [150]

POPE PIUS XI
(1922–1939)

Truly the spirit of expiation or reparation has always had the first and foremost place in the worship given to the Most Sacred Heart of Jesus, and nothing is more in keeping with the origin, the character, the power, and the distinctive practices of this form of devotion, as appears from the record of history and custom, as well as from the sacred liturgy and the acts of the Sovereign Pontiffs. For when Christ manifested Himself to Margaret Mary, and declared to her the infinitude of His love, at the same time, in the manner of a mourner, He complained that so many and such great injuries were done to Him by ungrateful men—and we would that these words in which He made this complaint were fixed in the minds of the faithful, and were never blotted out by oblivion: "Behold this Heart"—He said— "which has loved men so much and has loaded them with all benefits, and for this boundless love has had no return but neglect, and contumely, and this often from those who were bound by a debt and duty of a more special love." In order that these faults might be washed away, He then recommended several things to be done, and in particular the following as most pleasing to Himself, namely that men should approach the Altar with this purpose of expiating sin, making what is called a Communion of Reparation,—and that they should likewise make expiatory supplications and prayers, prolonged for a whole hour,—which is rightly called the "Holy Hour." These pious exercises have been approved by the Church and have also been enriched with copious indulgences. [151]

POPE PIUS XII
(1939–1958)

Just as the divine Redeemer, dying on the Cross, offered Himself as Head of the whole human race to the eternal Father, so also in this "clean oblation" (Mal 1:2), He, as Head of the Church, offers not only Himself but, in Himself, all His mystical members.[152]

In this manner [Eucharistic adoration] the faithful testify to and solemnly make evident the Faith of the Church according to which the Word of God and the Son of the Virgin Mary who suffered on the Cross, who lies present hidden in the Eucharist, and who reigns in heaven are believed to be identical.[153]

BLESSED JOSEMARÍA ESCRIVÁ
(1902–1975)

Consider what is most beautiful and most noble on earth, what pleases the mind and the other faculties, and what delights the flesh and the senses. Consider the world, and the other worlds that shine in the night —the whole universe.

And this, along with all the satisfied follies of the heart, is worth nothing, *is* nothing and less than nothing, compared with this God of mine!—of yours! Infinite treasure, most beautiful pearl . . . humbled, become a slave, reduced to nothingness in the form of a

servant in the stable where he willed to be born . . .
in Joseph's workshop, in his passion and in his igno-
minious death, and in the frenzy of Love—the blessed
eucharist![154]

"Treat him well for me, treat him well," said a certain
elderly bishop with tears in his eyes to the priests he
had just ordained.
 Lord, I wish I had the voice and the authority to
cry out in the same way to the ears and the hearts of
many, many Christians![155]

Receiving communion every day for so many years!
Anybody else would have been a saint by now—you
told me—and I . . . I'm always the same!
 Son, I replied, keep up your daily communion, and
think: What would I be if I hadn't received?[156]

Communion, union, communication, intimacy: Word,
bread, love.[157]

When you approach the tabernacle remember that *he*
has been waiting for you for twenty centuries.[158]

Piety has its own good manners. Learn them. It's a
shame to see those "pious" people who don't even
know how to assist at Mass—even those who hear it
daily—nor how to bless themselves (they make some
weird gestures very hurriedly), nor how to bend their
knee before the tabernacle (their ridiculous genuflec-
tions seem a mockery), nor how to bow their heads
reverently before an image of our Lady.[159]

It's true that I always call our tabernacle Bethany. Become a friend of the Master's friends—Lazarus, Martha, Mary—and then you will ask me no more why I call our tabernacle Bethany.[160]

I know you will be glad to have this prayer to the holy guardian angels of our tabernacles:

O angelic spirits, who guard our tabernacles, wherein lies the adorable treasure of the holy eucharist, defend it from profanation and preserve it for our love.[161]

If you don't keep in touch with Christ in prayer and in the bread, how can you make him known to others?[162]

POPE PAUL VI
(1897–1978)

He dwells with us full of grace and truth. He restores morality, nourishes the virtues, consoles the afflicted, strengthens the weak. He promises his own example to those who come to him that all may learn to be like himself, meek and humble of heart, and who seek not their own interests, but the things of God. Anyone, therefore, who approaches this august Sacrament with special devotion and endeavors to return generous love for Christ's own infinite love, experiences and fully understands, not without great spiritual joy and profit, how precious is the life hidden with Christ in God and how great is the converse with Christ, for there is nothing more consoling on earth, nothing more efficacious for advancing along the road to holiness.[163]

For if the sacred liturgy holds the first place in the life of the Church, the Eucharistic Mystery stands at the heart and center of the liturgy, since it is the font of life by which we are cleansed and strengthened to live not for ourselves but for God, and to be united in love among ourselves.[164]

To confirm what we have said by examples, it is not allowable to emphasize what is called the "communal" Mass to the disparagement of Masses celebrated in private, or to exaggerate the element of sacramental sign as if the symbolism, which all certainly admit in the Eucharist, expresses fully and exhausts completely the mode of Christ's presence in this sacrament. Nor is it allowable to discuss the mystery of transubstantiation without mentioning what the Council of Trent stated about the marvelous conversion of the whole substance of the bread into the Body and of the whole substance of the wine into the Blood of Christ, speaking rather only of what is called "transignification" and "transfiguration," or finally to propose and act upon the opinion according to which, in the Consecrated Hosts which remain after the celebration of the sacrifice of the Mass, Christ Our Lord is no longer present.[165]

It cannot be tolerated that any individual should on his own authority modify the formulas which were used by the Council of Trent to express belief in the Eucharistic Mystery. For these formulas, like the others which the Church uses to propose the dogmas of faith, express concepts which are not tied to a certain form of human culture, nor to a specific phase of human culture, nor to one or other theological school.

No, these formulas present that part of reality which necessary and universal experience permits the human mind to grasp and to manifest with apt and exact terms taken either from common or polished language. For this reason, these formulas are adapted to men of all times and all places. But the most sacred task of theology is, not the invention of new dogmatic formulas to replace old ones, but rather such a defense and explanation of the formulas adopted by the councils as may demonstrate that divine Revelation is the source of the truths communicated through these expressions.[166]

By means of the Mystery of the Eucharist, the Sacrifice of the Cross, which was once offered on Calvary, is remarkably re-enacted and constantly recalled, and its saving power exerted for the forgiveness of those sins which we daily commit.[167]

We should also mention "the public and social nature of every Mass," a conclusion which clearly follows from the doctrine we have been discussing. For even though a priest should offer Mass in private, that Mass is not something private; it is an act of Christ and of the Church. In offering this Sacrifice, the Church learns to offer herself as a sacrifice for all. Moreover, for the salvation of the entire world she applies the single, boundless, redemptive power of the Sacrifice of the Cross. For every Mass is offered not for the salvation of ourselves alone, but also for that of the whole world.[168]

VATICAN COUNCIL II
(1963)

The wonderful works of God among the people of the Old Testament were but a prelude to the work of Christ Our Lord in redeeming mankind by giving perfect glory to God. He achieved this task principally by the paschal mystery of his blessed passion, resurrection from the dead, and glorious ascension, whereby, "dying he destroyed our death, and rising he restored our life." For it was from the side of Christ as he slept the sleep of death upon the cross that there came forth "the wondrous sacrament of the whole Church."

Accordingly, just as Christ was sent by the Father so also he sent the apostles, filled with the Holy Spirit. This he did so that they might preach the Gospel to every creature and proclaim that the Son of God by his death and resurrection had freed us from the power of Satan and from death, and had brought us into the Kingdom of his Father. But he also willed that the work of salvation which they preached should be set in train through the sacrifice and the sacraments around which the entire liturgical life revolves. Thus by Baptism are men grafted into the paschal mystery of Christ; they die with him, are buried with him, and rise with him. They receive the spirit of adoption as sons "in which we cry, Abba, Father" (Rom 8:15) and thus become true adorers such as the Father seeks. In like manner as often as they eat the Supper of the Lord they proclaim the death of the Lord until he comes. That was why on the very day of Pentecost when the Church appeared before the world those "who received the word" of Peter "were baptized." And "they continued steadfastly in the teaching of the apostles and in the communion of the breaking of the bread and in prayers . . . praising God and being in favor with all people" (Acts 2:41–47). From that time onward the Church has never failed to come together to celebrate the paschal mystery, reading those things "which were in the scriptures concerning him" (Lk 24:27), celebrating the Eucharist in which "the victory and the triumph of his death are again made present," and at the same time giving thanks to God for his "inexpressible gift" (2 Cor 9:15) in Christ Jesus, "in praise of his glory" (Eph 1:12) through the power of the Holy Spirit.[169]

To accomplish so great a work Christ is always present in his Church, especially in her liturgical celebrations. He is present in the Sacrifice of the Mass not only in the person of his minister, "the same now offering, through the ministry of priests, who formerly offered himself on the cross," but especially in the eucharistic species. By his power he is present in the sacraments so that when anybody baptizes it is really Christ himself who baptizes. He is present in his word since it is he himself who speaks when the holy scriptures are read in the Church. Lastly, he is present when the Church prays and sings, for he has promised "where two or three are gathered together in my name there am I in the midst of them" (Mt 18:20).[170]

. . . The liturgy is the summit toward which the activity of the Church is directed; it is also the fount from which all her power flows. For the goal of the apostolic endeavor is that all who are made sons of God by faith and baptism should come together to praise God in the midst of his Church, to take part in the Sacrifice and to eat the Lord's Supper.

The liturgy, in its turn, moves the faithful "filled with the paschal sacraments" to be "one in holiness"; it prays that they "hold fast in their lives to what they have grasped by their faith." The renewal in the Eucharist of the covenant between the Lord and man draws the faithful and sets them aflame with Christ's insistent love. From the liturgy, therefore, and especially from the Eucharist, grace is poured forth upon us as from a fountain, and the sanctification of men in Christ and the glorification of God to which all the other activities of the Church are directed, as toward their end, are achieved with maximum effectiveness.[171]

At the Last Supper, on the night he was betrayed, our Savior instituted the eucharistic sacrifice of his Body and Blood. This he did in order to perpetuate the sacrifice of the Cross throughout the ages until he should come again, and so to entrust to his beloved Spouse, the Church, a memorial of his death and resurrection: a sacrament of love, a sign of unity, a bond of charity, a paschal banquet in which Christ is consumed, the mind is filled with grace, and a pledge for future glory is given to us.[172]

Union with Christ, which is the object of the sacrament, should extend to the whole Christian life. The faithful, therefore, being ever mindful of the gift they have received, should live their daily lives in a spirit of gratitude under the guidance of the Holy Spirit and thus derive more abundant fruits of charity.[173]

"The other sacraments, as indeed every ministry of the Church and every work of the apostolate, are linked with the Eucharist and directed toward it. For the Eucharist contains the entire spiritual good of the Church, namely, Christ himself, our Passover and living bread, offering through his flesh, living and life giving in the Spirit, life to men who are thus invited and led on to offer themselves, their labors, and all created things with him" (Decree on the Ministry and Life of Priests, 5).

The Eucharist both perfectly signifies and wonderfully effects that sharing in God's life and unity of God's people by which the Church exists. It is the summit of both the action by which God sanctifies the world in Christ, and the worship which men offer to Christ and which through him they offer to the Father in the Spirit. Its celebration "is the supreme means by which the faithful come to express in their lives and to manifest to others the mystery of Christ and the true nature of the Church" (SC 10).[174]

It is above all in the celebration of the mystery of unity that all Christians should be filled with sorrow at the divisions which separate them. They should therefore pray earnestly to God that all disciples of Christ may daily come closer to a proper understanding of the mystery of the Eucharist according to his mind, and may so celebrate it as to become sharers in the body of Christ, and so become one body (1 Cor 10:17) "linked by the very bonds by which he wishes it to be constituted."[175]

In this sacrament Christ is present in a unique way, whole and entire, God and man, substantially and permanently. This presence of Christ under the species "is called 'real' not in an exclusive sense, as if the other kinds of presence [i.e., in the faithful, the priest, and his word] were not real, but *par excellence*."[176]

As often as the sacrifice of the cross by which "Christ our Pasch is sacrificed" (1 Cor 5:7) is celebrated on the altar, the work of our redemption is carried out. Likewise, in the sacrament of the eucharistic bread, the unity of believers, who form one body in Christ (cf. 1 Cor 10:17), is both expressed and brought about. All men are called to this union with Christ, who is the light of the world, from whom we go forth, through whom we live, and towards whom our whole life is directed.[177]

The Eucharist, through which we do not cease to proclaim the death and resurrection of the Lord and to prepare ourselves for his coming again in glory, brings back constantly to mind the physical and moral sufferings by which Christ was afflicted, and which he had indeed freely accepted, even to his agony and death on the Cross. May the trials which you encounter be for you an opportunity for bearing in union with the Lord, and offering to the Father, the many misfortunes and unjust sufferings which weigh upon our brothers and sisters; to these the sacrifice of Christ can alone, in faith, give meaning.[178]

It is important that the mystery of the Eucharist should shine out before the eyes of the faithful in its true light. It should be considered in all its different aspects, and the real relationships which, as the Church teaches, are known to exist between these various aspects of the mystery should be understood by the faithful as to be reflected in their lives.[179]

What the faithful have received by faith and sacrament in the celebration of the Eucharist should have its effect on their way of life. They should seek to live joyfully and gratefully by the strength of this heavenly food, sharing in the death and resurrection of the Lord. And so everyone who has participated in the Mass should be "eager to do good works, to please God, and to live honestly, devoted to the Church, putting into practice what he has learnt, and growing in piety." He will seek to fill the world with the Spirit of Christ and "in all things, in the very midst of human affairs," to become a witness of Christ.[180]

No "Christian community can be built up unless it has as its basis and pivot the celebration of the holy Eucharist. It is from this therefore that any attempt to form a community must begin."[181]

"The Son of God in the human nature which he united to himself redeemed man and transformed him into a new creation by overcoming death through his own death and resurrection (cf. Gal 6:15; 2 Cor 5:17). For by giving his spirit he mystically established as his body his brethren gathered from all nations. In that body the life of Christ is communicated to those who believe; for through the sacraments they are joined in a mysterious but real way to the Christ who suffered and is glorified" (*Lumen Gentium* 7).

Therefore "Our Savior at the Last Supper on the night that he was betrayed instituted the eucharistic sacrifice of his Body and Blood so that he might perpetuate the sacrifice of the cross throughout the centuries till his coming. He thus entrusted to the Church, his beloved spouse, a memorial of his death and resurrection, a sacrament of love, a sign of unity, a bond of charity, a paschal meal in which Christ is eaten, the mind filled with grace, and a pledge of future glory given to us" (SC 47).[182]

The Mass, the Lord's Supper, is at the same time and inseparably:

— a sacrifice in which the sacrifice of the cross is perpetuated;

— a memorial of the death and resurrection of the Lord, who said, "Do this in memory of me" (Lk 22:19);

— a sacred banquet in which, through the communion of the Body and Blood of the Lord, the People of

God share the benefits of the Paschal Sacrifice, renew the New Covenant which God has made with
man once for all through the Blood of Christ, and
in faith and hope foreshadow and anticipate the es-
chatological banquet in the kingdom of the Father,
proclaiming the Lord's death "till his coming." [183]

In the Mass, therefore, the sacrifice and sacred meal
belong to the same mystery—so much so that they
are linked by the closest bond.

For in the sacrifice of the Mass Our Lord is immolated when "he begins to be present sacramentally as
the spiritual food of the faithful under the appearances
of bread and wine." It was for this purpose that Christ
entrusted this sacrifice to the Church, that the faithful
might share in it both spiritually, by faith and charity,
and sacramentally, through the banquet of Holy Communion. Participation in the Lord's Supper is always
communion with Christ offering himself for us as a
sacrifice to the Father. [184]

The celebration of the Eucharist that takes place at
Mass is the action not only of Christ, but also of the
Church. For in it Christ perpetuates in an unbloody
manner the sacrifice offered on the cross, offering himself to the Father for the world's salvation through the
ministry of priests. The Church, the spouse and minister of Christ, performs together with him the role of
priest and victim, offers him to the Father and at the
same time makes a total offering of herself together
with him. [185]

The celebration of the Eucharist in the sacrifice of the Mass is the origin and consummation of the worship shown to the Eucharist outside Mass. Not only are the sacred species which remain after the Mass derived from the Mass, but they are preserved so that those of the faithful who cannot come to Mass may be united to Christ, and his sacrifice celebrated in the Mass, through sacramental communion received with the right dispositions.[186]

The eucharistic sacrifice is the source and the summit of the whole of the Church's worship and of the Christian life. The faithful participate more fully in this sacrament of thanksgiving, propitiation, petition and praise, not only when they whole-heartedly offer the sacred victim, and in it themselves, to the Father with the priest, but also when they receive this same victim sacramentally.[187]

There should be no doubt in anyone's mind "that all the faithful ought to show this most holy sacrament the worship which is due to the true God, as has always been the custom of the Catholic Church. Nor is it to be adored any the less because it was instituted by Christ to be eaten." For even in the reserved sacrament he is to be adored because he is substantially present there through that conversion of bread and wine which, as the Council of Trent tells us, is most aptly named transubstantiation.

The mystery of the Eucharist should therefore be considered in all its fullness, not only in the celebration of the Mass but also in devotion to the sacred species which remain after Mass and are reserved to extend the grace of the sacrifice.[188]

When the faithful adore Christ present in the sacrament, they should remember that this presence derives from the sacrifice and is directed towards both sacramental and spiritual communion.

In consequence, the devotion which leads the faithful to visit the Blessed Sacrament draws them into an ever deeper participation of the Paschal Mystery. It leads them to respond gratefully to the gift of him who through his humanity constantly pours divine life into the members of his body. Dwelling with Christ our Lord, they enjoy his intimate friendship and pour out their hearts before him for themselves and for their dear ones, and pray for the peace and salvation of the world. They offer their entire lives with Christ to the Father in the Holy Spirit, and receive in this wonderful exchange an increase in faith, hope and charity. Thus they nourish those right dispositions which enable them with all true devotion to celebrate the memorial of the Lord and to receive frequently the bread given to us by the Father.

The faithful should therefore strive to worship Christ our Lord in the Blessed Sacrament, in harmony with their way of life. Pastors should exhort them to do this, and set them a good example.[189]

MOTHER TERESA OF CALCUTTA
(1910–1997)

Christ became the Bread of Life. But it seems that this act of self-giving wasn't enough for him. He wanted to give something more. He wanted to pass on to us the opportunity to give of ourselves to him, so we could turn our love for him into living deeds after eating the Bread of Life.[190]

Jesus is the Bread of Life that the Church offers me. Only through him, in him and with him can I live. He said, "If you do not eat my flesh and drink my blood, you will not have life within you." I know that he made himself the Bread of Life in order to satisfy my hunger for him and for his love. He, in turn, made himself the hungry one to satisfy my hunger for him through my love and service. He gives me the opportunity to feed him by feeding those who are hungry, to clothe him by clothing those who are naked, to heal him by caring for those who are sick, and to offer him shelter by housing those who are homeless and unwanted.[191]

As Missionaries of Charity we are especially called upon to see Christ in the appearance of bread and to touch him in the broken bodies of the poor.

Christ when he took bread said: "Take and eat, this is my body delivered for you." By giving himself, he invites us to grow in the power of his love to do what he has done.

Christ's love for us will give us strength and urge us to spend ourselves for him. "Let the sisters and the people eat you up." We have no right to refuse our life to others in whom we contact Christ.[192]

Like Mary, let us be in full zeal to go in haste to give Jesus to others. She was full of grace when, at the annunciation, she received Jesus. Like her, we too become full of grace every time we receive Holy Communion. It is the same Jesus whom she received and whom we receive at Mass. As soon as she received him she went with haste to give him to John. For us also, as soon as we receive Jesus in Holy Communion, let us go in haste to give him to our sisters, to our poor, the sick, to the dying, to the lepers, to the unwanted, and the unloved. By this we make Jesus present in the world today.[193]

We cannot separate our lives from the Eucharist; the moment we do, something breaks. People ask, "Where do the sisters get the joy and energy to do what they are doing?" The Eucharist involves more than just receiving; it also involves satisfying the hunger of Christ. He says, "Come to me." He is hungry for souls. Nowhere does the Gospel say: "Go away," but always, "Come to me."[194]

Our lives must be woven around the Eucharist. Ask Jesus to be with you, to work with you that you may be able to pray the work. You must really be sure that you have received Jesus. After that, you cannot give your tongue, your thoughts, or your heart to bitter-ness.

Put your sins in the chalice for the precious blood to wash away. One drop is capable of washing away the sins of the world.

The Eucharist is connected with the Passion. If Jesus had not established the Eucharist we would have for-gotten the crucifixion. It would have faded into the past and we would have forgotten that Jesus loved us. There is a saying that to be far away from the eyes is to be far away from the heart. To make sure that we do not forget, Jesus gave us the Eucharist as a memo-rial of his love. To make sure that we keep on loving him, he gives us his hunger (to satisfy our hunger for him)—he gives us the poorest of the poor.[195]

We must be faithful to the smallness of the Eucharist, that simple piece of bread which even a child can take in, that giving of a bath, that smile. . . . We have so much that we don't care about the small things. If we do not care, we will lose our grip on the Eucharist—on our lives. The Eucharist is so small.

I was giving Communion this morning. My two fin-gers were holding Jesus. Try to realize that Jesus allows himself to be broken. Make yourselves feel the need of each other. The passion and the Eucharist should open our eyes to that smallness: "This is my body; take and eat"—the small piece of bread. Today let us real-ize our own littleness in comparison with the Bread of Life.[196]

For us, we must never separate the Eucharist and the poor—or the poor and the Eucharist. You will really be a true Missionary of Charity when you go to the poor and take Jesus with you. He satisfied my hunger for him and now I go to satisfy his hunger for souls, for love.[197]

That is why Jesus made himself bread, to satisfy our hunger for God. See the humility of God. He also made himself the hungry one to satisfy our hunger for God through our love, our service. Let us pray that none of us will be unfaithful. Let us pray for our poor people. They are also hungry for God.[198]

Now more than ever we need to live out the teaching of Jesus: "Love one another, as the Father has loved me." We have to love as the Father loves his Son, Jesus, with the same mercy and compassion, joy and peace. Try to find out how the Father loves his Son, and then try to love one another in the same way. Find out in all humility how much you are loved by Jesus. From the time you realize you are loved by Jesus, love as he loves you.

In each of our lives Jesus comes as the Bread of Life —to be eaten, to be consumed by us. That is how he loves us. He also came as the Hungry One, hoping to be fed with the bread of our life, with our hearts that love and our hands that serve. In so doing, we prove that we have been created in the image and likeness of God, for God is love. When we love we are like God. This is what Jesus meant when he said, "Be perfect, as your heavenly Father is perfect."[199]

That you may know each other at the breaking of the bread, love each other in the eating of the Bread of Life, and serve each other and him in his poor by giving whole-hearted service.

When communicating with Christ in your heart—the partaking of the Living Bread—remember what Our Lady must have felt when the Spirit overpowered her and she, who was full of grace, became full with the body of Jesus. The Spirit in her was so strong that she immediately rose in haste to go and serve.

Each Holy Communion, each breaking of the Bread of Life, each sharing should produce in us the same, for it is the same Jesus who came to Mary and was made flesh. We, too, should be in haste to give this life of Jesus to our sisters and the poor.[200]

CODE OF CANON LAW
(1983)

The sacraments of the New Testament, instituted by Christ the Lord and entrusted to the Church, as they are the actions of Christ and the Church, stand out as the signs and means by which the faith is expressed and strengthened, worship is rendered to God and the sanctification of humankind is effected, and they thus contribute in the highest degree to the establishment, strengthening and manifestation of ecclesial communion; therefore both the sacred ministers and the rest of the Christian faithful must employ the greatest reverence and the necessary diligence in their celebration.[201]

The Most Holy Eucharist is the most august sacrament, in which Christ the Lord himself is contained, offered, and received, and by which the Church constantly lives and grows. The Eucharistic Sacrifice, the memorial of the death and resurrection of the Lord, in which the sacrifice of the cross is perpetuated over the centuries, is the summit and the source of all Christian worship and life; it signifies and effects the unity of the people of God and achieves the building up of the Body of Christ. The other sacraments and all the ecclesiastical works of the apostolate are closely related to the Holy Eucharist and are directed to it.[202]

The faithful are to hold the Eucharist in highest honor, taking part in the celebration of the Most August Sacrifice, receiving the sacrament devoutly and frequently, and worshiping it with supreme adoration; pastors, clarifying the doctrine on this sacrament, are to instruct the faithful thoroughly about this obligation.[203]

POPE JOHN PAUL II
(1980)

In reality, the ministerial and hierarchical priesthood, the priesthood of the Bishops and the priests, and, at their side, the ministry of the deacons—ministries which normally begin with the proclamation of the Gospel—are in the closest relationship with the Eucharist. The Eucharist is the principal and central *raison d'être* of the Sacrament of the priesthood, which effectively came into being at the moment of the institution of the Eucharist, and together with it. Not without reason the words "Do this in memory of me" are said immediately after the words of Eucharistic consecration, and we repeat them every time we celebrate the Holy Sacrifice.[204]

This worship, given therefore to the Trinity of the Father and of the Son and of the Holy Spirit, above all accompanies and permeates the celebration of the Eucharistic liturgy. But it must fill our churches also outside the timetable of Masses. Indeed, since the Eucharistic mystery was instituted out of love, and makes Christ sacramentally present, it is worthy of thanksgiving and worship. And this worship must be prominent in all our encounters with the Blessed Sacrament, both when we visit our churches and when the sacred species are taken to the sick and administered to them.[205]

Adoration of Christ in this Sacrament of love must also find expression *in various forms of Eucharistic devotion:* personal prayer before the Blessed Sacrament, hours of adoration, periods of exposition—short, prolonged and annual (Forty Hours)—Eucharistic benediction, Eucharistic processions, Eucharistic Congresses.[206]

The authentic sense of the Eucharist becomes of itself the school of active love for neighbor. We know that this is the true and full order of love that the Lord has taught us: "By this love you have for one another, everyone will know that you are my disciples." The Eucharist educates us to this love in a deeper way; it shows us, in fact, what value each person, our brother or sister, has in God's eyes, if Christ offers himself equally to each one, under the species of bread and wine. If our Eucharistic worship is authentic, it must make us grow in awareness of the dignity of each person. The awareness of that dignity becomes the *deepest motive of our relationship with our neighbor.*[207]

But we must always take care that this great meeting with Christ in the Eucharist does not become a mere habit, and that we do not receive him unworthily, that is to say, in a state of mortal sin. The practice of the virtue of penance and the Sacrament of Penance are essential for sustaining in us and continually deepening that spirit of veneration which man owes to God himself and to his love so marvelously revealed.[208]

In this Sacrament of bread and wine, of food and drink, *everything that is human really undergoes a singular transformation and elevation.* Eucharistic worship is not so much worship of the inaccessible transcendence as worship of the divine condescension, and it is also the merciful and redeeming transformation of the world in the human heart.[209]

The Church has a special duty to safeguard and strengthen the sacredness of the Eucharist. In our pluralistic and often deliberately secularized society, *the living faith* of the Christian community—a faith always aware of its rights vis-à-vis those who do not share that faith— ensures respect for this sacredness.[210]

The Eucharist is above all else a sacrifice. It is the sacrifice of the Redemption and also the sacrifice of the New Covenant, as we believe and as the Eastern Churches clearly profess: "Today's sacrifice", the Greek Church stated centuries ago, "is like that offered once by the Only-begotten Incarnate Word; it is offered by him (now as then), since it is one and the same sacrifice." Accordingly, precisely by making this single sacrifice of our salvation present, man and the world are restored to God through the paschal newness of Redemption. This restoration cannot cease to be: it is the foundation of the "new and eternal covenant" of God with man and of man with God. If it were missing, one would have to question both the excellence of the sacrifice of the Redemption, which in fact was perfect and definitive, and also the sacrificial value of the Mass. In fact, the Eucharist, being a true sacrifice, brings about this restoration to God.[211]

Consequently, the celebrant, as minister of this sacrifice, is the authentic *priest*, performing—in virtue of the specific power of sacred Ordination—a true sacrificial act that brings creation back to God. Although all those who participate in the Eucharist do not confect the sacrifice as he does, they offer with him, by virtue of the common priesthood, their own *spiritual sacrifices* represented by the bread and wine from the moment of their presentation at the altar. For this liturgical action, which takes a solemn form in almost all liturgies, has a "spiritual value and meaning." The bread and wine become in a sense a symbol of all that the Eucharistic assembly brings, on its own part, as an offering to God and offers spiritually.[212]

The encouragement and the deepening of Eucharistic worship are *proofs of that authentic renewal* which the Council set itself as an aim and of which they are *the central point*. And this, venerable and dear Brothers, deserves separate reflection. The Church and the world have great need for Eucharistic worship. Jesus waits for us in this Sacrament of love. Let us be generous with our time in going to meet him in adoration and in contemplation that is full of faith and ready to make reparation for the great faults and crimes of the world. May our adoration never cease.[213]

FATHER MARTIN LUCIA, SS.CC.

Even if you think you are the worst person in the world, remember that Jesus said that He has come not for the self-righteous and the well but for the sinners and those who are sick, as those "who are well do not need a physician". Or even if you think you are the worst prayer in the whole world and you can't even get through an "Our Father" without getting distracted, or if you sit or kneel for more than five or ten minutes and your mind goes in ten thousand different directions, Jesus wants you to know that He understands this. It is natural. What He wants you to understand is the supernatural: that He is so much in love with you that the mere fact that you choose to be with Him for a quiet hour every week brings indescribable delight to His Heart.[214]

Imagine the Pope inviting you to Rome to spend an hour with him; you would feel like the most important person in the world. Who would not see this as a great honor and do anything to get there? Yet it is a much greater honor to spend an hour with Jesus Himself. Those who kept company with Jesus in the Gospel stand out as men and women of great faith—they were His chosen friends who really believed in Him. They were ridiculed then, but are admired now. Those who keep company with Jesus in the Blessed Sacrament are His friends today who will stand out for all eternity for their faith in His Real Presence.[215]

Jesus hides His glory in the Blessed Sacrament that you may give Him glory by coming to Him in faith, and that you may love Him for Himself! He could fill every Catholic church 7 days a week, 24 hours a day by letting a single ray of His glory shine out. People would come from all over the world to see the miracle. But the miracle He wants us to see is the miracle of His divine love and humility where He Who created the whole world and Whom the whole world cannot contain, contains Himself in the Blessed Sacrament for love of us, to be our Divine Companion during our pilgrimage through life. To be our Good Shepherd who leads us to life-giving waters, to be our Divine Physician who comes to heal the lonely and the brokenhearted.[216]

On Praying the Rosary
before the Blessed Sacrament

When we pray the Rosary in front of the Blessed Sacrament, we love Jesus with the Heart of Mary. When we pray the Rosary in front of Jesus in the Blessed Sacrament, we offer to Jesus the perfect adoration of Mary.

We unite our love for Jesus to the perfect love and praise of Mary. Jesus receives our holy hour as if Mary herself were making it, because no matter how weak our faith or poor our love, Mary encloses us in her Heart and Jesus accepts our hour with Him as coming directly from the heart of His very own Mother. The Immaculate Heart of Mary repairs and makes up for what is lacking in our own heart.

The fifteen mysteries of the Rosary are related and centered in the one central mystery of our faith, the Holy Eucharist, where "the work of our redemption is accomplished." The Eucharist continues and makes present the fifteen mysteries of the Holy Rosary.

When we come to the Eucharist, we come to Bethlehem, for the Eucharist is the continuation of Christ's incarnation on earth. This is the theme of the Joyful Mysteries. Living the Joyful Mysteries: the obedience of Mary, the trust, the adoration, the consecration, are what bring joy to our soul.

When we come to the Eucharist, we come to Calvary, for here Jesus renews His perfect sacrifice on the Cross and continues to immolate Himself for love of us, where "the victory and triumph of His death are again made present." The Eucharist is the fruit of our Lord's Passion. This is the theme for the Sorrowful Mysteries. The four ends of the Mass, adoration, thanksgiving, reparation and petition, are continued in the Blessed Sacrament for here "Jesus lives to make intercession for us."

By His Holy Wounds, which are now the glory of Paradise, we are healed in this Holy Sacrament of all our wounds of mind, heart, and soul. Here is where we are renewed by the power of His grace flowing from His Holy Wounds which are forever fresh with the life-giving waters of His Divine Love. The five external wounds of Jesus represent His five interior wounds, (see 53rd chapter of Isaiah). By these wounds, we are healed.

When we come to the Eucharist, we come to the Resurrection, for this is where the Risen Savior dwells! He is the Lamb on the throne who shepherds us. The Eucharist is a foretaste of Heaven and a foreshadowing of the future glory that awaits us, where we will love God with God's very own love. This is the theme of the Glorious Mysteries. In union with the Sacred Hearts of Jesus and Mary, we re-live these mysteries in our daily life, for where Jesus went, His Bride, the Church, must follow. Before we are glorified with Him forever, we too must pick up our cross daily and follow Him.[217]

CATECHISM OF THE CATHOLIC CHURCH
(1994)

The Eucharist—Source and Summit of Ecclesial Life

"The Eucharist is the efficacious sign and sublime cause of that communion in the divine life and that unity of the People of God by which the Church is kept in being. It is the culmination both of God's action sanctifying the world in Christ and of the worship men offer to Christ and through him to the Father in the Holy Spirit" (Congregation of Rites, instruction, *Eucharisticum mysterium*, 6).[218]

Finally, by the Eucharistic celebration we already unite ourselves with the heavenly liturgy and anticipate eternal life, when God will be all in all (cf. 1 Cor 15:28).[219]

In brief, the Eucharist is the sum and summary of our faith: "Our way of thinking is attuned to the Eucharist, and the Eucharist in turn confirms our way of thinking" (Saint Irenaeus, *Adv. haeres.* 4, 18, 5: PG 7/1, 1028).[220]

What Is This Sacrament Called?

The inexhaustible richness of this sacrament is expressed in the different names we give it. Each name evokes certain aspects of it. It is called:

Eucharist, because it is an action of thanksgiving to God. The Greek words *eucharistein* (cf. Lk 22:19; 1 Cor 11:24) and *eulogein* (cf. Mt 26:26; Mk 14:22) recall the Jewish blessings that proclaim—especially during a meal—God's works: creation, redemption, and sanctification.[221]

The Lord's Supper, because of its connection with the supper which the Lord took with his disciples on the eve of his Passion and because it anticipates the wedding feast of the Lamb in the heavenly Jerusalem (cf. 1 Cor 11:20; Rev 19:9).

The *Breaking of Bread*, because Jesus used this rite, part of a Jewish meal, when as master of the table he blessed and distributed the bread (cf. Mt 14:19; 15:36; Mk 8:6, 19), above all at the Last Supper (cf. Mt 26:26; 1 Cor 11:24). It is by this action that his disciples will recognize him after his Resurrection (cf. Lk 24:13–35), and it is this expression that the first Christians will use to designate their Eucharistic assemblies (cf. Acts 2:42, 46; 20:7, 11); by doing so they signified that all who eat the one broken bread, Christ, enter into communion with him and form but one body in him (cf. 1 Cor 10:16–17).

The *Eucharistic assembly* (*synaxis*), because the Eucharist is celebrated amid the assembly of the faithful, the visible expression of the Church (cf. 1 Cor 11:17–34).[222]

The *memorial* of the Lord's Passion and Resurrection.

The *Holy Sacrifice*, because it makes present the one sacrifice of Christ the Savior and includes the Church's offering. The terms *holy sacrifice of the Mass*, "*sacrifice of praise*", *spiritual sacrifice*, *pure and holy sacrifice* are also used (Heb 13:15; cf. 1 Pet 2:5; Ps 116:13, 17; Mal 1:11), since it completes and surpasses all the sacrifices of the Old Covenant.

The *Holy and Divine Liturgy*, because the Church's whole liturgy finds its center and most intense expression in the celebration of this sacrament; in the same sense we also call its celebration the *Sacred Mysteries*. We speak of the *Most Blessed Sacrament* because it is the Sacrament of sacraments. The Eucharistic species reserved in the tabernacle are designated by this same name.[223]

Holy Communion, because by this sacrament we unite ourselves to Christ, who makes us sharers in his Body and Blood to form a single body (cf. 1 Cor 10:16–17). We also call it: *the holy things* (*ta hagia*; *sancta*) (*Apostolic Constitutions* 8, 13, 12: PG 1, 1108; *Didachē* 9, 5; 10:6: SCh 248, 176–78)—the first meaning of the phrase "communion of saints" in the Apostles' Creed—the *bread of angels*, *bread from heaven*, *medicine of immortality* (Saint Ignatius of Antioch, *Ad Eph.* 20, 2: SCh 10, 76), *viaticum*. . . .[224]

Holy Mass (*Missa*), because the liturgy in which the mystery of salvation is accomplished concludes with the sending forth (*missio*) of the faithful, so that they may fulfill God's will in their daily lives.[225]

The Sacramental Sacrifice: Thanksgiving, Memorial, Presence

THANKSGIVING AND PRAISE TO THE FATHER

The Eucharist, the sacrament of our salvation accomplished by Christ on the cross, is also a sacrifice of praise in thanksgiving for the work of creation. In the Eucharistic sacrifice the whole of creation loved by God is presented to the Father through the death and the Resurrection of Christ. Through Christ the Church can offer the sacrifice of praise in thanksgiving for all that God has made good, beautiful, and just in creation and in humanity.[226]

The Eucharist is a sacrifice of thanksgiving to the Father, a blessing by which the Church expresses her gratitude to God for all his benefits, for all that he has accomplished through creation, redemption, and sanctification. Eucharist means first of all "thanksgiving."[227]

The Eucharist is also the sacrifice of praise by which the Church sings the glory of God in the name of all creation. This sacrifice of praise is possible only through Christ: he unites the faithful to his person, to his praise, to his intercession, so that the sacrifice of praise to the Father is offered *through* Christ and *with* him, to be accepted *in* him.[228]

Various Prayers from Throughout the Centuries

ACTS OF SPIRITUAL COMMUNION

My Jesus, I believe that Thou art present in the Blessed Sacrament. I love Thee above all things and I desire Thee in my soul. Since I cannot now receive Thee sacramentally, come at least spiritually into my heart. As though Thou wert already there, I embrace Thee and unite myself wholly to Thee; permit not that I should ever be separated from Thee. [Saint Alphonsus Liguori][229]

At Thy feet, O my Jesus, I prostrate myself, and I offer Thee the repentance of my contrite heart, which is humbled in its nothingness and in Thy holy presence. I adore Thee in the Sacrament of Thy love, the ineffable Eucharist. I desire to receive Thee into the poor dwelling that my heart offers Thee. While waiting for the happiness of sacramental Communion, I wish to possess Thee in spirit. Come to me, O my Jesus, since I, for my part, am coming to Thee! May Thy love embrace my whole being in life and in death. I believe in Thee, I hope in Thee, I love Thee. Amen. [Raphael Cardinal Merry del Val]

I believe that Thou, O Jesus, art in the Most Holy Sacrament! I love Thee and desire Thee! Come into my heart. I embrace Thee; oh, never leave me!

PRAYERS TO THE
MOST BLESSED SACRAMENT

My Lord Jesus Christ, who, for the love You bear us, remain night and day in this Sacrament, full of compassion and love, awaiting, calling and welcoming all who come to visit You. I believe that You are present in the Sacrament of the Altar. I adore You from the abyss of my nothingness, and I thank You for all of the graces that You have given to me until now, and in particular, for having given me Yourself in this Sacrament, for having given me Your Most Holy Mother Mary as my advocate and for having called me to visit You in this church.

I now salute Your Most Loving Heart, and this for three ends: first, in thanksgiving for this great gift; second, to make amends to You for all the outrages which You receive in this Sacrament from all Your enemies; third, I intend by this visit to adore You in all the places on earth in which You are the least revered and most abandoned.

My Jesus, I love You with my whole heart. I grieve for having until now so many times offended Your infinite goodness. I propose, by Your grace, never more to offend You for the time to come; and now, miserable and unworthy though I am, I consecrate myself to You without reserve. I give You and renounce my entire will, my affections, my desires, and all that I possess. From now on, use me and all that I have as You wish. All I ask of You and desire is Your holy love, final perseverance, and the perfect accomplishment of Your will.

I recommend to You the souls in Purgatory; but especially those who had the greatest devotion to the Most Blessed Sacrament and to the Most Blessed Virgin Mary. I also recommend to You all poor sinners.

And finally, my dear Savior, I unite all my affections with the affections of Your Most Loving Heart, and I offer them with You to Your Eternal Father and beg Him for Your sake and for love of You graciously to accept and grant them.

Give me, good Lord, a full faith and a fervent charity, a love of you, good Lord, incomparably above the love of myself; and that I love nothing to your displeasure but everything in an order to you.

Take from me, good Lord, this lukewarm fashion, or rather cold manner of meditation and this dullness praying to you. And give me warmth, delight and life in thinking about you. And give me your grace to long for your holy sacraments and specially to rejoice in the presence of your blessed Body, sweet Savior Christ, in the Holy Sacrament of the Altar, and duly to thank you for your precious coming. [Saint Thomas More]

ACT OF FAITH IN
THE DIVINE EUCHARIST

I believe in my heart and openly profess that the bread and wine which are placed upon the altar are by the mystery of the sacred prayer and the words of the Redeemer substantially changed into the true and life-giving Flesh and Blood of Jesus Christ Our Lord and after the Consecration there is present the true Body of Christ which was born of the Virgin Mary and offered up for the salvation of the world, hung upon the Cross, and now sits at the right hand of the Father and there is present the true Blood of Christ which flowed from his side. They are present not only by means of a sign and of the efficacy of the Sacrament, but also in the very reality and truth of their nature and substance. Amen. [Saint Gregory VII]

O my God, I firmly believe that Thou art really and corporally present in the Blessed Sacrament of the altar. I adore Thee here present from the very depths of my heart, and I worship Thy sacred presence with all possible humility. O my soul, what joy to have Jesus Christ always with us, and to be able to speak to Him, heart to heart, with confidence. Grant, O Lord, that I, having adored Thy divine Majesty here on earth in this wonderful Sacrament, may be able to adore It eternally in heaven. Amen.[230]

A PRAYER TO FOSTER THE PRACTICE OF DAILY COMMUNION

O sweetest Jesu, Thou who camest into the world to give all souls the life of Thy grace, and who, to preserve and nourish it in them, hast willed to be at once the daily cure of their daily infirmities and their daily sustenance; we humbly beseech Thee, by Thy Heart all on fire with love for us, to pour forth upon them all Thy divine Spirit, so that those who are unhappily in mortal sin, may turn to Thee and regain the life of grace which they have lost, and those who, through Thy gift, are already living this divine life, may draw near daily, when they can, to Thy sacred table, whence, by means of daily Communion, they may receive daily the antidote of their daily venial sins, and may every day foster within themselves the life of grace; and being thus ever more and more purified, may come at last to the possession of that eternal life which is happiness with Thee. Amen.[231]

Behold, O my most loving Jesus, how far Thine exceeding love hath reached! Of Thine own Flesh and Most Precious Blood Thou hast prepared for me a divine table in order to give Thyself wholly to me. What hath impelled Thee to such transports of Love? Nothing else surely save Thy most loving Heart. O adorable Heart of my Jesus, burning furnace of divine charity, receive my heart within Thy most sacred wound; to the end that in this school of love, I may learn to make a return of love to the God who hath given me such wondrous proofs of His love. Amen.[232]

DESIRE FOR CLOSER UNION

Lord Jesus Christ, pierce my soul with your love so that I may always long for you alone, who are the bread of angels and the fulfillment of the soul's deepest desires. May my heart always hunger and feed upon you so that my soul may be filled with the sweetness of your presence. May my soul thirst for you, who are the source of life, wisdom, knowledge, light and all the riches of God our Father. May I always seek and find you, think upon you, speak to you and do all things for the honor and glory of your holy name. Be always my only hope, my peace, my refuge and my help in whom my heart is rooted so that I may never be separated from you. [Saint Bonaventure]

SPIRITUAL COMMUNION

CHRIST:

My child, receive Me in Holy Communion as often as you are able. Try to purify your motives, so that you may eventually come to Me without any selfish consideration, but only from a desire to please Me and to be with Me. When you have risen to this high spiritual level, I shall grant to you many special graces which you have not yet experienced.

One of these graces is the thirst for supernatural love. Your desire to be united with Me will grow stronger and stronger. You will reach the point where you will wish to receive Me more than once a day. Not being able to do so sacramentally, you will turn to spiritual communion as a remedy for your spiritual thirst.

With faith and love you will turn to Me frequently throughout the day, asking Me to come to you as through Holy Communion. Through spiritual communion you will seek to imitate My sacramental visit in some small way. For the brief moments at your disposal you will speak to Me, listen to Me, and act as though I had come to you in Holy Communion.

Though spiritual communion can never replace nor equal My sacramental presence, it is an excellent method of prayer. It is very pleasing to Me and will bring you many extra blessings throughout the day. I shall teach you to shut out the world around you for a while. You will learn to be more aware of My nearness in your daily activities. You will appreciate My friendship more deeply because you took the trouble to come closer to Me.

THINK:

Though there is no real substitute for the Blessed Sacrament, I can make frequent spiritual communions to satisfy my spiritual thirst in some small way. When I ask our Lord to come to me in a spiritual communion, He is pleased and grants me many extra graces. Spiritual communion will help me come closer to Jesus in my daily life. Yes, through this method of prayer I can join my heart to Christ's as often as I choose. This is one desire with which Jesus will cooperate every time.

PRAY:

My Jesus, close companion of my soul, I am tired of forgetting You in my daily activities. Though You are present in Heaven, here on earth You are also present in various, less perfect ways. In the Blessed Sacrament You are supernaturally present in Your divine and human natures, just as when You walked on earth. Then, by sanctifying grace You are present in my soul in a different manner. When You come to me in Holy Communion, Your union with me becomes stronger and more active. Your human nature binds me more securely to Your divinity. Your precious body and blood act like food within my soul, helping me live Your life more perfectly. Though spiritual communion is a very imperfect and incomplete substitute for Holy Communion, You are pleased at my desire to be united to You once again. Since You also desire to see me live in constant union with You, You will grant me wonderful graces each time I make an effort to come closer to You through spiritual communion. I hope to make this effort more often as I go through my daily occupations and activities. Amen. [233]

VISITS TO THE BLESSED SACRAMENT

CHRIST:

My child, if My true presence on the altar were limited to one place alone, many people from all parts of the world would try to visit that place at some time or other in their lives. Yet, now that I have made it easy for all to come to Me, see how many visit Me only when they are obliged!

Many people are so cold toward Me. Like children they are impressed only by what they can touch and see. I have given them their greatest treasure in the Blessed Sacrament. Through My Apostles and their successors, I have promised to be personally present wherever the Blessed Sacrament is. Make every effort to be deeply impressed by this greatest of all earthly gifts.

It is not enough for you to believe in My real presence upon the altar. I placed Myself there for love of you. I wanted to be near you in some visible way, so that you might visit Me as often as you wished. You should wish it as often as possible.

People come to Me for different reasons. Some come only on Sundays and holy days, through a sense of obligation. Either they do not want to lose Heaven, or they desire My help in their daily life. Then there are those who come to Me through mere habit. They act automatically, without any particular devotion to Me. There are, however, a certain number who come to Me for the best reason. They come to Me because they are glad to be near Me. These people please Me best of all. They receive many extra graces which are not granted to others.

Consider how devoted My saints were to Me. They seized every opportunity to visit Me and stay with Me. They desired to abandon all useless interests so that they might have more time with Me. In return for this generosity with Me, they received a clearer understanding of My boundless goodness and a deeper appreciation of My infinite love.

You, too, have the opportunity to give Me more of your time and attention. Make a greater effort to come closer to Me in friendship. You have the privilege of kneeling before Me like the simple, wonderful shepherds; the tired, admiring Magi; the suffering, begging leper; the penitent, hopeful Magdalene; the convicted, converted Thomas. How are you taking advantage of this privilege?

How much easier it will be for you to face Me in your judgment if you have loved to face Me often during your earthly life. Each visit to Me is an act of faith, of love, and of self-purification. Come to Me often, so that I may shower more of My gifts upon your soul.

THINK:

One who neglects Jesus in the Blessed Sacrament hurts himself more than he realizes. By frequent visits I come closer to that wonderful union with God which He desires to grant me in my daily life. Each visit can bring me closer to Him in true friendship. I need no special formula, no particular prayers, no unusual requirements. All that I need is to present myself before Him, talking if I so wish, listening if I am so disposed, or simply staying with Him. He is more interested in me than in anyone else. Though I may feel very dull, He is interested in my thoughts, my desires, my needs, hopes, ambitions, efforts, and labors. My daily life is a matter of highest importance to Him. He is glad to see me come because each visit gives Him another excuse to grant me more blessings. He is there for love of me. I ought to visit Him often for love of Him.

PRAY:

My Jesus, truly present in the Blessed Sacrament, I have not shown You half of the appreciation which I owe You. Grant me the grace to grow in this appreciation. You deserve far more attention than I have shown You. How often could I come to you with a slight effort or even inconvenience to myself! Yet, I fail to do so. I do not treat my human friends half so neglectfully as I treat You. This sacrament is a living proof of Your love for me. I hope to show my love for You by a greater devotion toward You from now on. You will see me more than just once a week. As often as I am reasonably able, I shall visit You. I want to give You more of my attention, my time, my interest, and my life. Amen.[234]

O BOUNDLESS CHARITY!

O boundless charity! Just as you gave yourself, wholly God and wholly human, so you left all of yourself as food so that while we are pilgrims in this life we might not collapse in our weariness but be strengthened by you, Heavenly Food.

O mercenary people! And what has your God left you? He has left you himself, wholly God and wholly human, hidden under the whiteness of this bread.

O fire of love! Was it not enough to gift us with creation in your image and likeness, and to create us anew in your Son's Blood, without giving us yourself as food, the whole of divine being, the whole of God? What drove you? Nothing but your charity, mad with love as you are! [Saint Catherine of Siena]

WHAT FOOD IS THIS?

And what food is this? Food of angels, supreme eternal purity! This is why you want and demand such purity of the soul who receives this most sweet Sacrament—such purity that if it were possible for the angelic nature to be purified (a nature that has no need for purification), such a great mystery would demand that it be purified. And how shall the soul be purified? In the fire of your charity and by the washing of her face in the Blood of your only begotten Son. O my wretched soul! How dare you approach such a great mystery without purification? Blush for shame, you who deserve to live with the beasts and the devils because you have always acted like a beast and followed the devil's will. [Saint Catherine of Siena]

PRAYER OF SAINT AMBROSE
BEFORE MASS

Lord Jesus Christ, I approach Thy banquet table in fear and trembling, for I am a sinner and dare not rely on my own worth but only on Thy goodness and mercy. I am defiled by my many sins in body and soul and by my unguarded thoughts and words. Gracious God of majesty and awe, I seek Thy protection, I look for Thy healing. Poor troubled sinner that I am, I appeal to Thee, the fountain of all mercy. I cannot bear Thy judgment, but I trust in Thy salvation. Lord, I show my wounds to Thee and uncover my shame before Thee. I know my sins are many and great, and they fill me with fear, but I hope in Thy mercies, for they cannot be numbered. Lord Jesus Christ, Eternal King, God and man, crucified for mankind, look upon me with mercy and hear my prayer, for I trust in Thee. Have mercy on me, full of sorrow and sin, for the depth of Thy compassion never ends. Praise to Thee, saving sacrifice, offered on the wood of the cross for me and for all mankind. Praise to the noble and precious Blood, flowing from the wounds of my crucified Lord Jesus Christ and washing away the sins of the whole world. Remember, Lord, Thy creature, whom

Thou hast redeemed with Thy blood; I repent my sins, and I long to put right what I have done. Merciful Father, take away all my offenses and sins; purify me in body and soul, and make me worthy to taste the Holy of Holies. May Thy Body and Blood, which I intend to receive, although I am unworthy, be for me the remission of my sins, the washing away of my guilt, the end of my evil thoughts, and the rebirth of my better instincts. May it incite me to do the works pleasing to Thee and profitable to my health in body and soul, and be a firm defense against the wiles of my enemies. Amen.

PRAYER TO THE BLESSED VIRGIN MARY BEFORE MASS

Mother of mercy and love, Blessed Virgin Mary, I am a poor and unworthy sinner, and I turn to thee in confidence and love. As thou stoodst by thy Son as He hung dying on the cross, stand also by me, a poor sinner, and by all the priests who are offering Mass today here and throughout the entire Church. Help us to offer a perfect and acceptable sacrifice in the sight of the holy and undivided Trinity, our most high God. Amen.

PRAYER TO SAINT JOSEPH
BEFORE MASS

O Blessed Joseph, happy man, to whom it was given not only to see and to hear that God Whom many kings longed to see, and saw not, to hear, and heard not; but also to carry Him in your arms, to embrace Him, to clothe Him, and guard and defend Him.

℣. Pray for us, O Blessed Joseph.
℟. *That we may be made worthy of the promises of Christ.*

O God, Who hast given us a royal priesthood, we beseech Thee, that as Blessed Joseph was found worthy to touch with his hands, and to bear in his arms, Thine only begotten Son, born of the Virgin Mary, so may we be made fit, by cleanness of heart and blamelessness of life, to minister at Thy holy altar; may we, this day, with reverent devotion partake of the Sacred Body and Blood of Thine only begotten Son, and may we in the world to come be accounted worthy of receiving an everlasting reward. Through the same Christ our Lord. Amen.

PRAYER BEFORE COMMUNION

O Lord Jesus Christ, Son of the living God, Who by the will of the Father and with the cooperation of the Holy Spirit hast by Thy death given life unto the world: Deliver me by this, Thy most sacred Body and Blood, from all my sins and from every evil. Make me always cling to Thy commandments and never permit me to be separated from Thee. Amen.

PRAYER BEFORE THE RECEPTION OF THE EUCHARIST

O Lord Jesus Christ, Son of the Living God, who according to the will of the Father and with the cooperation of the Holy Spirit hast by Thy death given life unto the world, I adore and revere this Thy holy Body and this Thy holy Blood which was given over and poured forth for the many unto the remission of sins. O merciful Lord, I beg of Thy mercy that through the power of this sacrament Thou wilt make me one of that many. Through faith and love make me feel the power of these sacraments so I may experience their saving power. Absolve and free from all sin and punishment of sin Thy servants, Thy handmaidens, myself, all who have confessed their sins to me, those whom I have promised or am obliged to pray for, and so too those who themselves hope or beg to be helped by my prayers with Thee. Make our Church rejoice in Thy constant protection and consolation. Amen. [Saint Anselm]

PRAYER TO SAINT
PETER JULIAN EYMARD

O Saint Peter Julian, who received the great privilege of so perfectly knowing what treasures are ours in the Most Blessed Sacrament, of being all afire with seraphic love for It, and of consecrating unto It your untiring zeal that It might be perpetually adored and glorified by all mankind, we beg of you to obtain for us the spiritual and the temporal favors of which we stand in need.

Obtain for us particularly to become, in imitation of you, faithful adorers in spirit and truth of the Most Blessed Sacrament, while tending ever more toward the acquiring of Christian Virtue, above all, of sincere humility. Thus we hope to live that life of union with Our Lord which was the aim of your constant zeal, as it is the principal effect of Holy Communion in our souls.

Finally, O Saint Peter Julian, obtain for us your own filial devotion toward Our Lady of the Most Blessed Sacrament, that we may learn from that dear Divine Mother how to serve and adore on earth Our Savior hidden in His Sacrament, and thus come to adore and glorify Him unveiled in Heaven. Amen.

PRAYER TO OUR LADY OF
THE MOST BLESSED SACRAMENT

O Virgin Mary, Our Lady of the Most Blessed Sacrament, who art the glory of Christians, the joy of the universal Church, and the hope of the world, pray for us. Kindle in all the faithful a lively devotion to the most Holy Eucharist, so that they may all be made worthy to receive Holy Communion every day.

Our Lady of the Most Blessed Sacrament, pray for us.

OFFERING OF A HOLY HOUR

My most kind Jesus, I desire during this hour to "watch" with Thee, and by the love of my poor heart to console Thee for the bitter sorrow which overwhelmed Thee in the Garden of Gethsemane. I desire to forget myself and all that concerns me excepting my sins, the foresight of which caused Thee so much suffering in Thine agony, and as I was the cause of sorrow to Thee then, so now I desire to be to Thee a consolation. . . . I offer Thee, moreover, this hour of prayer and reparation for the triumph of the Church, for the conversion of souls and nations, and for every other intention for which Thou didst pray, sweat blood, endure Thine agony, and accept Thy bitter passion and death. Angel of the agony, help me so to pass this Holy Hour that I may console the Heart of my Jesus and promote His interests throughout the world.

NIGHT SALUTATION AND PRAYER TO JESUS IN THE TABERNACLE

O Divine Jesus, lonely tonight in so many tabernacles, without visitor or worshipper, I offer Thee my heart. Oh, may its very beating be a prayer of love to Thee! Thou art ever watching under the sacramental veils. In Thy love Thou never sleepest, and Thou art never weary of Thy vigils for sinners. O loving Jesus, O lonely Jesus, may my heart be a lamp, the light of which shall burn and beam for Thee alone! Watch, Sacramental Sentinel, watch, for the weary world, for the erring soul, and for Thy poor child!

O Sacrament most holy! O Sacrament divine! All praise and all thanksgiving be every moment Thine!

PRAYER TO JESUS IN THE SACRAMENT OF THE ALTAR

Dear Jesus, present in the Sacrament of the Altar, be forever thanked and praised. Love, worthy of all celestial and terrestrial love, Who, out of infinite love for me, ungrateful sinner, didst assume our human nature, didst shed Thy most Precious Blood in the cruel scourging, and didst expire on a shameful cross for our eternal welfare! Now, illumined with lively faith, with the outpouring of my whole soul and the fervor of my heart, I humbly beseech Thee, through the infinite merits of Thy painful sufferings, give me the strength and courage to destroy every evil passion which sways my heart, to bless Thee in my greatest affliction, to glorify Thee by the exact fulfillment of all my duties, supremely to hate all sin, and thus to become a saint.

THANKSGIVING
TO THE HOLY TRINITY

Eternal Father, I thank Thee for the gift that Thou hast given me. It is Thy beloved Son, in Whom Thou art well pleased. In Him and by Him give me strength to keep all my good resolutions.

Eternal Son, I thank Thee for the gift Thou hast given me. It is Thyself Who didst die for me. Make me, dear Jesus, wiser with Thy heavenly wisdom and show me clearly all the things I should do for God.

Eternal Spirit, I thank Thee for the gift Thou hast given me. It is Jesus, whose soul Thou didst sanctify with Thy holiest treasures.

Make me, dear Spirit, more loving, that I may cling more closely to God.

O ever-blessed Trinity, three Persons in one God, help me to live according to this gift of gifts which I have received at the altar of Jesus.

ACTS OF PREPARATION AND THANKSGIVING FOR COMMUNION

1. Act of Preparation

Almighty and everlasting God, behold I come to the Sacrament of Thine only begotten Son, Our Lord Jesus Christ: I come as one infirm to the physician of life, as one unclean to the fountain of mercy, as one blind to the light of everlasting brightness, as one poor and needy to the Lord of heaven and earth. Therefore I implore the abundance of Thy measureless bounty that Thou wouldst vouchsafe to heal my infirmity, wash my uncleanness, enrich my poverty and clothe my nakedness, that I may receive the Bread of Angels, the King of kings, the Lord of lords, with such reverence and humility, with such sorrow and devotion, with such purity and faith, with such purpose and intention as may be profitable to my soul's salvation. Grant unto me, I pray, the grace of receiving not only the Sacrament of our Lord's Body and Blood, but also the grace and power of the Sacrament. O Most gracious God, grant me so to receive the body of Thine only begotten Son, Our Lord Jesus Christ, which he took from the Virgin Mary, as to merit to be incorporated into His mystical Body and to be numbered amongst His members. O most loving Father, give me the grace to behold forever Thy beloved Son with His face at last unveiled, whom I now purpose to receive under the sacramental veil here below.

2. Thanksgiving

I give Thee thanks, holy Lord, Father almighty, everlasting God, Who has vouchsafed to feed me, a sinner, Thine unworthy servant, for no merits of my own, but only out of the goodness of Thy great mercy, with the precious Body and Blood of Thy Son, our Lord Jesus Christ; and I pray Thee, that this holy Communion may be to me, not guilt for punishment, but a saving intercession for pardon. Let it be to me an armor of faith and a shield of good will. Let it be to me a casting out of vices; a driving away of all evil desires and fleshly lusts; an increase in charity, patience, humility, obedience, and all virtues; a firm defense against the plots of all my enemies, both seen and unseen; a perfect quieting of all motions of sin, both in my flesh and in my spirit; a firm cleaving unto Thee, the only and true God, and a happy ending to my life. And I pray Thee to deign to bring me, a sinner, to that ineffable Feast, where Thou art with Thy Son and the Holy Ghost, art to Thy holy ones true light, full satisfaction, everlasting joy, consummate pleasure and perfect happiness. Amen. [Saint Thomas Aquinas]

ACT OF REPARATION

Most sweet Jesus, whose overflowing charity for men is requited by so much forgetfulness, negligence and contempt, behold us prostrate before Thee, eager to repair by a special act of homage the cruel indifference and injuries to which Thy loving Heart is everywhere subject. Mindful, alas! that we ourselves have had a share in such great indignities, which we now deplore from the depths of our hearts, we humbly ask Thy pardon and declare our readiness to atone by voluntary expiation, not only for our own personal offenses, but also for the sins of those who, straying far from the path of salvation, refuse in their obstinate infidelity to follow Thee, their Shepherd and Leader, or, renouncing the promises of their baptism, have cast off the sweet yoke of Thy law. We are now resolved to expiate each and every deplorable outrage committed against Thee; we are now determined to make amends for the manifold offenses against Christian modesty in unbecoming dress and behavior, for all the foul seductions laid to ensnare the feet of the innocent, for the frequent violations of Sundays and holy days, and the shocking blasphemies uttered against Thee and Thy Saints. We wish also to make amends for the insults to which Thy Vicar on earth and Thy priests are subjected, for the profanation, by conscious neglect or terrible acts of sacrilege, of the very crimes of nations who resist the rights and teaching authority of the Church which Thou hast founded. Would that we were able to wash away such abominations with our blood. We now offer, in reparation for these violations of Thy divine honor, the satisfaction Thou once made to Thy Eternal Father on the cross and which Thou continuest to renew daily on our altars; we offer it in union with the acts of atonement of Thy Virgin Mother and all the

Saints and of the pious faithful on earth; and we sincerely promise to make recompense, as far as we can with the help of Thy grace, for all neglect of Thy great love and for the sins we and others have committed in the past. Henceforth, we will live a life of unswerving faith, of purity of conduct, of perfect observance of the precepts of the Gospel and especially that of charity. We promise to the best of our power to prevent others from offending Thee and to bring as many as possible to follow Thee. O loving Jesus, through the intercession of the Blessed Virgin Mother, our model in reparation, deign to receive the voluntary offering we make of this act of expiation; and by the crowning gift of perseverance keep us faithful unto death in our duty and the allegiance we owe to Thee, so that we may all one day come to that happy home, where with the Father and the Holy Spirit Thou livest and reignest, God, forever and ever. Amen.

AN ACT OF ADORATION
AND REPARATION

I adore Thee profoundly, O my Jesus, in Thy sacramental form; I acknowledge Thee to be true God and true Man, and by this act of adoration I intend to atone for the coldness of so many Christians who pass before Thy churches and sometimes before the very Tabernacle in which Thou art pleased to remain at all hours with loving impatience to give Thyself to Thy faithful people, and do not so much as bend the

knee before Thee, and who, by their indifference proclaim that they grow weary of this heavenly manna,
like the people of Israel in the wilderness. I offer Thee
in reparation for this grievous negligence, the Most
Precious Blood which Thou didst shed from Thy five
wounds, and especially from Thy sacred Side, and entering therein, I repeat a thousand times with true rec-
ollection of spirit:

O Sacrament most holy! O Sacrament divine!
All praise and all thanksgiving be every moment Thine!

Our Father, Hail Mary, Glory be.

Profoundly I adore Thee, my Jesus; I acknowledge
Thy presence in the Blessed Sacrament, and by this
act of adoration I intend to atone for the carelessness
of so many Christians who see Thee carried to poor
sick people to strengthen them for the great journey to
eternity, and leave Thee unescorted, nay, who scarcely
give Thee any outward marks of reverence. I offer
Thee in reparation for such coldness, the Most Precious Blood which Thou didst shed from Thy five
wounds and especially from Thy sacred Side, and entering therein I say again and again with my heart full
of devotion:

O Sacrament most holy! O Sacrament divine!
All praise and all thanksgiving be every moment Thine!

Our Father, Hail Mary, Glory be.

Profoundly I adore Thee, my Jesus, true Bread of life eternal, and by my adoration I intend to compensate Thee for the many wounds which Thy Heart suffers daily in the profaning of churches where Thou art pleased to dwell beneath the sacramental veils to be adored and loved by all Thy faithful people; and in reparation for so many acts of irreverence, I offer Thee the Most Precious Blood which Thou didst shed from Thy five wounds and especially from Thy sacred Side, and entering therein with recollected spirit I repeat every instant:

O Sacrament most holy! O Sacrament divine!
All praise and all thanksgiving be every moment Thine!

Our Father, Hail Mary, Glory be.

Profoundly I adore Thee, my Jesus, the living Bread which cometh down from heaven, and by this act of adoration, I intend to atone for all the many acts of irreverence which are committed all the day long by Thy faithful when they assist at Holy Mass, wherein through Thine exceeding love Thou dost renew in an unbloody manner the self-same sacrifice which Thou didst once offer on Calvary for our salvation. I offer Thee in atonement for such base ingratitude the Most Precious Blood which Thou didst shed from Thy five wounds and especially from Thy sacred Side, and entering therein with sincere devotion, I unite my voice to that of the Angels who stand around Thee in adoration, saying with them:

O Sacrament most holy! O Sacrament divine!
All praise and all thanksgiving be every moment Thine!

Our Father, Hail Mary, Glory be.

Profoundly I adore Thee, my Jesus, true Victim of expiation for our sins, and I offer Thee this act of adoration to atone for the sacrilegious outrages Thou dost suffer from so many ungrateful Christians who dare to draw near to receive Thee with mortal sin upon their souls. In reparation for such hateful sacrileges I offer Thee the last drops of Thy Most Precious Blood, which Thou didst shed from Thy sacred wounds and especially from the wound in Thy sacred Side, and entering therein with a devout heart, I adore Thee, I bless and I love Thee, and I repeat with all the hearts who are devoted to the Blessed Sacrament:

O Sacrament most holy! O Sacrament divine!
All praise and all thanksgiving be every moment Thine!

Our Father, Hail Mary, Glory be.[235]

PRAYER OF SAINT CAJETAN

Look down, O Lord, from Thy sanctuary, from Thy dwelling in heaven on high, and behold this sacred Victim which our great High Priest, Thy holy Son our Lord Jesus Christ, offers up to Thee for the sins of His brethren and be appeased despite the multitude of our transgressions. Behold, the voice of the Blood of Jesus, our Brother, cries to Thee from the cross.

Give ear, O Lord. Be appeased, O Lord. Hearken and do not delay for Thine own sake, O my God; for Thy Name is invoked upon this city and upon Thy people and deal with us according to Thy mercy. Amen.

PRAYER FROM AKITA, JAPAN

Most Sacred Heart of Jesus,
Truly present in the Holy Eucharist,
I consecrate my body and soul
To be entirely one with Your Heart
Being sacrificed at every instant
On all the altars of the world
And giving praise to the Father,
Pleading for the coming of His Kingdom.

Please receive this humble offering of myself.
Use me as You will for the glory of the Father
and the salvation of souls.

Most Holy Mother of God,
Never let me be separated from your Divine Son.
Please defend and protect me as your special child.
Amen.

FATIMA PRAYERS

My God, I believe, I adore, I hope, and I love You.
I ask forgiveness for those who do not believe, nor adore, nor hope, nor love You.

Most Holy Trinity, Father, Son and Holy Ghost, I adore You profoundly, and I offer You the Most Precious Body, Blood, Soul, and Divinity, of Jesus Christ, present in all the tabernacles of the world, in reparation for the outrages, sacrileges, and indifferences by which He is offended, and by the infinite merits of His Most Sacred Heart and through the Immaculate Heart of Mary, I beg the conversion of poor sinners.

Hail, saving Victim, offered for me and for all mankind upon the gibbet of the Cross.

Hail, precious Blood, flowing from the wounds of our crucified Lord Jesus Christ, and washing away the sins of the whole world.

Be mindful, O Lord, of Your creature, whom You have redeemed with Your Precious Blood.

ANIMA CHRISTI (1)

Soul of my Savior, sanctify my breast;
Body of Christ, be thou my saving guest;
Blood of my Savior, bathe me in thy tide,
Wash me with water flowing from thy side.

Strength and protection may thy passion be;
O blessed Jesus, hear and answer me;
Deep in thy wounds, Lord, hide and shelter me;
So shall I never, never part from thee.

Guard and defend me from the foe malign;
In death's dread moments make me only thine;
Call me and bid me come to thee on high,
When I may praise thee with thy saints for aye.

ANIMA CHRISTI (2)

Soul of Christ, sanctify me.
Body of Christ, save me.
Blood of Christ, inebriate me.
Water from the side of Christ, wash me.
Passion of Christ, strengthen me.
O good Jesus, hear me
Within thy wounds, hide me.
Suffer me not to be separated from thee.
From the malignant Enemy, defend me.
In the hour of my death, call me.
And bid me come to thee.
That with thy saints I may praise thee.
Forever and ever. Amen.

A PRAYER FOR PRIESTS

Keep them, I pray Thee, dearest Lord,
   Keep them, for they are Thine—
Thy priests whose lives burn out before
   Thy consecrated shrine.
Keep them, for they are in the world,
   Though from the world apart;
When earthly treasures tempt, allure,—
   Shelter them in Thy heart.
Keep them and comfort them in hours
   Of loneliness and pain,
When all their life of sacrifice
   For souls seems but in vain.

Keep them, and O remember, Lord,
  They have no one but Thee,
Yet they have only human hearts,
  With human frailty.
Keep them as spotless as the Host,
  That daily they caress;
Their every thought and word and deed,
  Deign, dearest Lord, to bless.

PRAYER OF SAINT CATHERINE
OF SIENA FOR PRIESTS

Father, receive also the one who has given me Communion in the precious Body and Blood of your Son. Strip him of himself and free him from himself; clothe him in your eternal will and bind him to yourself with a knot which can never be undone, so that he may be a fragrant plant in the garden of the Church.

SUPPORT FOR FAMILIES

O Living Bread, that came down from heaven to give life to the world! O loving shepherd of our souls, from your throne of glory whence, a "hidden God", you pour out your grace upon families and peoples, we commend to you particularly the sick, the unhappy, the poor and all who beg for food and employment, imploring for all and every one the assistance of your providence; we commend to you the families, so that they may be fruitful centers of Christian life. May the abundance of your grace be poured over all. [Pope John XXIII]

FOOD FOR SERVICE

O Jesus, present in the sacrament of the altar, teach all the nations to serve you with willing hearts, knowing that to serve God is to reign. May your sacrament, O Jesus, be light to the mind, strength to the will, joy to the heart. May it be the support of the weak, the comfort of the suffering, the wayfaring bread of salvation for the dying and for all the pledge of future glory. Amen. [Pope John XXIII]

O BREAD OF HEAVEN

O bread of heaven, beneath this veil
Thou dost my very God conceal:
My Jesus, dearest treasure, hail;
I love Thee and adoring kneel;
Each loving soul by Thee is fed
With Thy own self in form of bread.

O food of life, Thou who dost give
The pledge of immortality
I live; no 'tis not I that live;
God gives me life, God lives in me:
He feeds my soul, He guides my ways,
And every grief with joy repays.

O bond of love, that dost unite
The servant to his living Lord;
Could I dare live, and not requite
Such love,—then death were meet reward:
I cannot live unless to prove
Some love for such unmeasured love.

O mighty fire, that dost burn
To kindle every mind and heart,
For Thee my frozen soul doth yearn:
Come, Lord of love, Thy warmth impart.
If thus to speak too bold appear,
'Tis love like Thine has banished fear.

O sweetest dart of love divine
If I have sinned, then vengeance take:
Come pierce this guilty heart of mine.
And let it die for His dear sake
Who once expired on Calvary,
His heart pierced through for love of me.

My dearest good, Who dost so bind
My heart with countless chains to Thee,
O sweetest love, my soul shall find
In Thy dear bonds true liberty;
Thyself Thou hast bestowed on me,
Thine, Thine forever I will be!

Beloved Lord in heaven above,
There, Jesus, Thou awaitest me;
To gaze on Thee with changeless love;
Yes, thus, I hope, thus shall it be:
For how can He deny me heaven

Who here on earth Himself has given?
[Saint Alphonsus Liguori]

MY SOUL WHAT DOST THOU?

My soul, what dost thou? Answer me—
　　Love God, who loves thee well:—
Love only does he ask of thee,
　　Canst thou his love repel?

See, how on earth for love of thee,
　　In lowly form of bread,
The sovereign good and majesty
　　His dwelling-place has made.

He bids thee now his friendship prove,
　　And at his table eat;
To share the bread of life and love,
　　His own true flesh thy meat.

What other gift so great, so high,
　　Could God himself impart?
Could love divine do more to buy
　　The love of thy poor heart?

Though once, in agonies of pain,
　　Upon the cross he died,
A love so great, not even then
　　Was wholly satisfied.

Not till the hour when he had found
　　The sweet, mysterious way

To join his heart in closest bond
   To thy poor heart of clay.

How, then, amid such ardent flame,
   My soul, dost thou not burn?
Canst thou refuse, for very shame,
   A loving heart's return?

Then yield thy heart, at length, to love
   That God of charity,
Who gives his very self to prove
   The love he bears to thee.
[Saint Alphonsus Liguori]

THE MYSTERY OF LOVE

You loved me from all eternity,
therefore you created me.
You loved me after you had made me,
therefore you became man for me.
You loved me after you became man for me,
therefore you lived and died for me.
You loved me after you had died for me,
therefore you rose again for me.
You loved me after you had risen for me,
therefore you went to prepare a place for me.
You loved me after you had gone to prepare a
place for me,
therefore you came back to me.
You loved me after you came back to me,

therefore you desired to enter into me and be
united to me.
This is the meaning of the Blessed Sacrament.
The mystery of love.
[Archbishop Goodier]

PANGE LINGUA

Of the glorious body telling,
O, my tongue, its mysteries sing,
And the Blood all price excelling,
Which the world's eternal king,
In a noble womb once dwelling,
Shed for this world's ransoming.

Given for us, for us descending
Of a virgin to proceed,
Man with man in converse blending,
Scattered he the Gospel seed,
Till his sojourn drew to ending,
Which he closed in wondrous deed.

At the last great supper lying
Circled by his brethren's band,
Meekly with the law complying,
First he finished its command,
Then, immortal food supplying,
Gave himself with his own hand.

Word made flesh, by word he maketh
Very bread his flesh to be;

Man in wine Christ's blood partaketh:
And if senses fail to see.
Faith alone the true heart waketh
To behold the mystery.

Therefore we, before him bending
This great sacrament revere;
Types and shadows have their ending,
For the newer rite is here;
Faith, our outward sense befriending,
Makes the inward vision clear.

Glory let us give, and blessing
To the Father, and the Son;
Honor, might, and praise addressing,
While eternal ages run;
Ever to his love confessing,
Who, from both, with both is one.
[Saint Thomas Aquinas]

PANIS ANGELICUS

Panis angelicus fit panis hominum;
Dat panis coelicus figuris terminum:
O res mirabilis!
Manducat Dominum
Pauper, servus et humilis.
Te Trina Deitas unaque poscimus,
Sic nos Tu visita, sicut Te colimus.
Per Tuas semitas duc nos quo tendimus,
Ad lucem quam inhabitas.

The angels' bread becomes man's bread.
Heaven's bread does away with symbols.
O Wonder!
He feeds upon his Lord, the poor
And the lowly servant does.
You God, Three and One,
Visit us as we pray to You.
By Your footsteps guide us as we journey
To the light where You live.

FOOD OF TRAVELERS

O food of travelers, angels' bread
Manna wherewith the blessed are fed,
Come nigh and with Thy sweetness fill
The hungry hearts that seek Thee still.

O fount of love, O well unpriced,
Outpouring from the heart of Christ,
Give us to drink of very Thee,
And all we pray shall answered be.

O Jesus Christ we pray to Thee
That this Thy presence which we see,
Though now in form of bread concealed,
To us may be in heaven revealed.
[*Maintzisch Gesangbuch*]

SACRUM CONVIVIUM
(Praise of Communion)

O sacred banquet, in which Christ is received,
The offering of his passion renewed,
The mind is filled with grace,
And a promise of future glory is given to us!

LAUDA SION
(Praise of the Blessed Sacrament)

Holy Church now praise your Savior,
He is your King and Shepherd too,
  So praise in songs and hymns.

O praise with all your strength and power,
For he is greater than all praise
  Nor can you praise enough.

Remember now his special gift;
The living bread which gives us life
  Today is set before us.

No doubt at all remains with us,
At table seated with the twelve,
  He gave his loving gift.

Let praise be all complete and loud,
Let hearts be full of joyful praise,
  In gladness and respect.

We honor now this glorious day,
And always will recall with love,
    The gift he gave us then.

At table our new-found king,
New paschal meal of new-given law
    Put end to all before.

The new law put old to flight,
The truth now chased the darkness cold,
    The light brought end to night.

What Christ then did at this great meal,
He ordered us to do today,
    That we remember him.

Obedient to his loving words,
We consecrate the bread and wine,
    In sacrifice for sin.

The teaching given Christians is,
The bread into his body is changed,
    The wine into his blood.

We cannot understand or see,
But living faith now makes us firm,
    Beyond all nature's laws.

Appearances not real, but signs
Of what lies hidden underneath,
    Where priceless gift we find.

For food to flesh and drink to blood
Is changed; yet Christ complete remains,
    'Neath each appearance true.

He's never broken when received,
He's not divided, torn apart,
   But comes to us entire.

Received by thousands or by one,
By being received he's not destroyed,
   And each receives the same.

Both just and sinners can receive,
But fruits are not the same in each,
   It brings both life and death.

The just get life, the sinners death,
A very different effect,
   Though both received alike.

And when we break the sign of bread,
Remember then and do not doubt,
The same is now in each small part,
   As first the whole contained.

We don't divide our Savior Christ,
We break the covering sign alone,
The glory or the state of Christ,
   Is not made less at all.

Behold the Bread for angels fit,
Is made the food of mortal men,
It's God's true bread to feed his sons,
   No good for those in sin.

In figures long ago foretold,
When Paschal Lamb the chosen saved,
When Isaac once was sacrificed,
   And manna fed the Jews.

Jesus, Shepherd, Bread most true,
Have mercy now on us your own,
Defend us all and care for us,
And grant that we'll your goodness see
In everlasting life.

God, you know and rule all things;
You feed us men while here on earth;
In heaven let us share your feast,
Let's be your friends and heirs with you
In homeland of the saints.

AVE VERUM CORPUS
(Hail to Thee, True Body)

Hail to thee, true body born
From the Virgin Mary's womb!
The same that on the cross was nailed
And bore for man the bitter doom.

Thou, whose side was pierced and flowed
Both with water and with blood;
Suffer us to taste of thee,
In our life's last agony.

O kind, O loving one!
O sweet Jesus, Mary's Son!

O SAVING VICTIM

O saving Victim! opening wide
The gate of heaven to man below!
Our foes press on from every side:
Thine aid supply, Thy strength bestow.
To Thy great Name be endless praise,
Immortal Godhead, One in Three!
Oh, grant us endless length of days,
In our true native land with Thee. Amen.

VERY BREAD

Very Bread, good Shepherd, tend us,
Jesu, of Thy love befriend us,
Thou refresh us, Thou defend us,
Thine eternal goodness send us
In the land of life to see.
Thou Who all things canst and knowest,
Who on earth such food bestowest,
Grant us with Thy Saints though lowest,
Where the heavenly feast Thou shewest,
Fellow-heirs and guests to be. Amen.

SHORT PRAYERS

O Jesus in the Blessed Sacrament, have mercy on us!

Praise and adoration ever more be given to the most holy Sacrament.

O Sacrament most holy, O Sacrament divine!
All praise and all thanksgiving be every moment Thine!

I adore Thee every moment,
O living Bread from heaven,
Great Sacrament!

Blessed is He that cometh in the name of the Lord;
Hosanna in the highest!

Hail, true Body born of Mary the Virgin!

Jesus, My God, I adore Thee here present in the Sacrament of Thy love!

Lord, I am not worthy that Thou shouldst enter under my roof; but only say the word and my soul shall be healed.

The Body of Our Lord Jesus Christ preserve my soul unto everlasting life. Amen.

LITANY OF THE MOST
PRECIOUS BLOOD OF JESUS
(*for private use only*)

Lord, have mercy on us.
Christ, have mercy on us.
Lord, have mercy on us. Christ, hear us,
Christ graciously hear us.
God, the Father of Heaven,
have mercy on us.
God, the Son, Redeemer of the world,
have mercy on us.
God, the Holy Spirit,
have mercy on us.
Holy Trinity, One God,
have mercy on us.

Blood of Christ, only-begotten Son of the Eternal
Father,
save us.
Blood of Christ, Incarnate Word of God,
save us.
Blood of Christ, of the New and Eternal Testament,
etc.
Blood of Christ, falling upon the earth in the Agony,
Blood of Christ, shed profusely in the Scourging,
Blood of Christ, flowing forth in the Crowning with
Thorns,
Blood of Christ, poured out on the Cross,

Blood of Christ, Price of our salvation,
Blood of Christ, without which there is no
　　forgiveness,
Blood of Christ, Eucharistic drink and refreshment
　　of souls,
Blood of Christ, River of mercy,
Blood of Christ, Victor over demons,
Blood of Christ, Courage of martyrs,
Blood of Christ, Strength of confessors,
Blood of Christ, bringing forth virgins,
Blood of Christ, Help of those in peril,
Blood of Christ, Relief of the burdened,
Blood of Christ, Solace in sorrow,
Blood of Christ, Hope of the penitent,
Blood of Christ, Consolation of the dying,
Blood of Christ, Peace and Tenderness of hearts,
Blood of Christ, Pledge of Eternal Life,
Blood of Christ, freeing souls from Purgatory,
Blood of Christ, most worthy of all glory and honor,

Lamb of God, Who takest away the sins of the world,
　　spare us, O Lord.
Lamb of God, Who takest away the sins of the world,
　　graciously hear us, O Lord.
Lamb of God, Who takest away the sins of the world,
　　have mercy on us.

℣. Thou hast redeemed us, O Lord, in Thy Blood.
℟. *And made of us a kingdom for our God.*

Let us pray:

Almighty and eternal God, Thou hast appointed Thine only-begotten Son the Redeemer of the world, and willed to be appeased by His Blood. Grant, we beseech Thee, that we may worthily adore this Price of our salvation, and through its power be safeguarded from the evils of this present life, so that we may rejoice in its fruits forever in Heaven. Through this same Christ our Lord. Amen.[236]

LITANY OF
THE BLESSED SACRAMENT
(*for private use only*)

Lord, have mercy on us.
Christ, have mercy on us.
Lord, have mercy on us. Christ, hear us,
Christ graciously hear us.
God, the Father of Heaven,
have mercy on us.
God, the Son, Redeemer of the world,
have mercy on us.
God, the Holy Spirit,
have mercy on us.
Holy Trinity, One God,
have mercy on us.

Living Bread, that came down from Heaven,
have mercy on us.

Hidden God and Saviour,
  have mercy on us
Wheat of the elect,
  etc.
Wine of which virgins are the fruit,
Bread of fatness and royal dainties,
Perpetual Sacrifice,
Clean oblation,
Lamb without spot,
Most pure feast,
Food of angels,
Hidden manna,
Memorial of the wonders of God,
Super-substantial Bread,
Word made Flesh, dwelling in us,
Sacred Host,
Chalice of benediction,
Mystery of Faith,
Most high and adorable Sacrament,
Most holy of all sacrifices,
True Propitiation for the living and the dead,
Heavenly antidote against the poison of sin,
Most wonderful of all miracles,
Most holy Commemoration of the Passion of Christ,
Gift transcending all fullness,
Special Memorial of divine love,
Affluence of divine bounty,
Most august and holy Mystery,
Medicine of immortality,
Tremendous and life-giving Sacrament,
Bread made Flesh by the omnipotence of the Word,

Unbloody Sacrifice,
At once our Feast and our Guest,
Sweetest banquet, at which angels minister,
Sacrament of piety,
Bond of charity,
Priest and Victim,
Spiritual Sweetness tasted in its proper source,
Refreshment of holy souls,
Viaticum of such as die in the Lord,
Pledge of future glory,

Be merciful, *spare us, O Lord.*
Be merciful, *graciously hear us, O Lord.*

From an unworthy reception of Thy Body and Blood,
   O Lord, deliver us.
From the lust of the flesh,
   O Lord deliver us.
From the lust of the eyes,
   etc.
From the pride of life,
From every occasion of sin,
Through the desire with which Thou didst long to
    eat this Passover with Thy disciples,
Through that profound humility with which Thou
    didst wash their feet,
Through that ardent charity by which Thou didst
    institute this Divine Sacrament,
Through Thy Precious Blood, which Thou didst
    leave us upon our altars,
Through the five wounds of this Thy most holy
    Body, which Thou didst receive for us.

We sinners beseech Thee, *hear us.*

That Thou wilt preserve and increase our faith, reverence, and devotion toward this admirable Sacrament, *we beseech Thee, hear us.*

That Thou wilt conduct us, through true confession of our sins, to a frequent reception of the Holy Eucharist, *we beseech Thee, hear us.*

That Thou wilt deliver us from all heresy, perfidy, and blindness of heart, *we beseech Thee, hear us.*

That Thou wilt impart to us the precious and heavenly fruits of this most holy Sacrament, *we beseech Thee, hear us.*

That at the hour of our death Thou wilt strengthen and defend us by this heavenly Viaticum, *we beseech Thee, hear us.*

Son of God, *we beseech Thee, hear us.*

Lamb of God, Who takest away the sins of the world, *spare us, O Lord.*

Lamb of God, Who takest away the sins of the world, *graciously hear us, O Lord.*

Lamb of God, Who takest away the sins of the world, *have mercy on us.*

℣. Christ hear us.

℟. *Christ graciously hear us.*

℣. Thou didst give them Bread from Heaven. Alleluia.

℟. *Containing in Itself all sweetness. Alleluia.*

Let us pray:

O God, Who in this wonderful Sacrament hast left us a memorial of Thy Passion, grant us the grace, we beseech Thee, so to venerate the Sacred Mysteries of Thy Body and Blood, that we may ever continue to feel within ourselves the blessed fruit of Thy Redemption, Who livest and reignest, God forever and ever. Amen.[237]

LITANY FOR HOLY COMMUNION

(for private use only)

Lord, have mercy on us.
  Christ, have mercy on us.
Lord, have mercy on us. Christ, hear us,
  Christ graciously hear us.
God, the Father of Heaven,
  have mercy on us.
God, the Son, Redeemer of the world,
  have mercy on us.
God, the Holy Spirit,
  have mercy on us.
Holy Trinity, One God,
  have mercy on us.

Jesus, living Bread, which came down from Heaven,
  have mercy on us.
Jesus, Bread from Heaven giving life to the world,
  have mercy on us.

Jesus, hidden God and Saviour,
   etc.
Jesus, Who hast loved us with an everlasting love,
Jesus, Whose delights are to be with the children
   of men,
Jesus, Who hast given Thy Flesh for the life of
   the world,
Jesus, Who invitest all to come to Thee,
Jesus, Who promisest eternal life to all that receiveth
   Thee,
Jesus, Who with desire desirest to eat this Pasch
   with us,
Jesus, ever ready to receive and welcome us,
Jesus, Who standest at our door knocking,
Jesus, Who hast said that if we will open to Thee
   the door, Thou wilt come in and sup with us,
Jesus, Who receivest us into Thy arms and blessest us
   with the little children,
Jesus, Who sufferest us to sit at Thy feet with
   Magdalen,
Jesus, Who invitest us to lean upon Thy bosom
   with the beloved disciple,
Jesus, Who hast not left us orphans,
Most dear Sacrament,
Sacrament of Love,
Sacrament of sweetness,
Life-giving Sacrament,
Sacrament of strength,
My God and my all,

That our hearts may pant after Thee as the hart after the fountains of water,
we beseech Thee, hear us.

That Thou wouldst manifest Thyself to us as to the two disciples in the breaking of bread,
we beseech Thee, hear us.

That we may know Thy voice like Magdalen,
etc.

That with a lively faith we may confess with the beloved disciple, "It is the Lord,"

That Thou wouldst bless us who have not seen and yet have believed,

That we may love Thee in the Blessed Sacrament with our whole heart, with our whole soul, with all our mind, and with all our strength,

That the fruit of each Communion may be fresh love,

That our one desire may be to love Thee and to do Thy will,

That we may ever remain in Thy love,

That Thou wouldst teach us how to receive and welcome Thee,

That Thou wouldst teach us how to pray, and Thyself to pray within us,

That with Thee every virtue may come into our souls,

That throughout this day Thou wouldst keep us closely united to Thee,

That Thou wouldst give us grace to persevere to the end,

That Thou wouldst be our support and Viaticum,

That with Thee and leaning on Thee we may safely
  pass through all dangers,

That our last act may be one of perfect love and our
  last breath a long deep sigh to be in Our Father's
  house,

That Thy sweet face may smile upon us when we appear before Thee,

That our banishment from Thee, dearest Lord, may
  not be very long,

That when the time is come, we may fly up from our
  prison to Thee, and in Thy Sacred Heart find our
  rest forever,

Lamb of God, Who takest away the sins of the world,
  spare us, O Lord.

Lamb of God, Who takest away the sins of the world,
  graciously hear us, O Lord.

Lamb of God, Who takest away the sins of the world,
  have mercy on us.

℣. Stay with us, Lord, because it is toward evening,
℟. *And the day is now far spent.*

Let us pray:

We come to Thee, dear Lord, with the Apostles, saying, "Increase our faith." Give us a strong and lively
faith in the mystery of Thy Real Presence in the midst
of us. Give us the splendid faith of the centurion,
which drew from Thee such praise. Give us the faith
of the beloved disciple to know Thee in the dark and

say, "It is the Lord!" Give us the faith of Martha to confess, "Thou art the Christ, the Son of the living God." Give us the faith of Magdalen to fall at Thy feet crying, "Rabboni, Master." Give us the faith of all Thy Saints, to whom the Blessed Sacrament hast been Heaven begun on earth. In every Communion increase our faith; for with faith, love and humility and reverence and all good will come into our souls. Dearest Lord, increase our faith. Amen.[238]

LITANY OF REPARATION TO OUR LORD IN THE BLESSED EUCHARIST
(for private use only)

Lord, have mercy on us.
  Christ, have mercy on us.
Lord, have mercy on us. Christ, hear us,
  Christ graciously hear us.
God, the Father of Heaven,
  have mercy on us.
God, the Son, Redeemer of the world,
  have mercy on us.
God, the Holy Spirit,
  have mercy on us.
Holy Trinity, One God,
  have mercy on us.

Sacred Host, offered for the salvation of sinners,
  have mercy on us.

Sacred Host, annihilated on the altar for us and by us,
have mercy on us.
Sacred Host, despised by lukewarm Christians,
etc.
Sacred Host, mark of contradiction,
Sacred Host, insulted by blasphemers,
Sacred Host, Bread of angels, given to animals,
Sacred Host, flung into the mud and trampled
underfoot,
Sacred Host, dishonored by unfaithful priests,
Sacred Host, forgotten and abandoned in Thy churches,

Be merciful unto us,
pardon us, O Lord.
Be merciful unto us,
hear us, O Lord.

For the outrageous contempt of this most wonderful
Sacrament,
we offer Thee our reparation.
For Thine extreme humiliation in Thine admirable
Sacrament,
we offer Thee our reparation.
For all unworthy Communions,
etc.
For the irreverences of wicked Christians,
For the profanation of Thy sanctuaries,
For the holy ciboriums dishonored and carried away
by force,
For the continual blasphemies of impious men,
For the obduracy and treachery of heretics,

For the unworthy conversations carried on in Thy holy temples,

For the profaners of Thy churches which they have desecrated by their sacrileges,

That it may please Thee to increase in all Christians the reverence due to this adorable Mystery,
we beseech Thee, hear us.

That it may please Thee to manifest the Sacrament of Thy love to heretics,
we beseech Thee, hear us.

That it may please Thee to grant us the grace to atone for their hatred by our burning love for Thee,
etc.

That it may please Thee that the insults of those who outrage Thee may rather direct them against ourselves,

That it may please Thee graciously to receive this our humble reparation,

That it may please Thee to make our adoration acceptable to Thee,

Pure Host, *hear our prayer.*
Holy Host, *hear our prayer.*
Immaculate Host, *hear our prayer.*

Lamb of God, Who takest away the sins of the world, *spare us, O Lord.*

Lamb of God, Who takest away the sins of the world, *graciously hear us, O Lord.*

Lamb of God, Who takest away the sins of the world,
  have mercy on us.

Lord, have mercy on us.
Christ, have mercy on us.

℣. See, O Lord, our affliction,
℟. *And give glory to Thy Holy Name.*

Let us pray:

O Lord Jesus Christ, Who dost deign to remain with us in Thy wonderful Sacrament to the end of the world, in order to give to Thy Father, by the memory of Thy Passion, eternal glory, and to give to us the Bread of life everlasting: Grant us the grace to mourn, with a heart full of sorrow, over the injuries which Thou hast received in this adorable Mystery, and over the many sacrileges which are committed by the impious, by heretics and by bad Catholics.

Inflame us with an ardent zeal to repair all these insults to which, in Thine infinite mercy, Thou hast preferred to expose Thyself rather than deprive us of Thy Presence on our altars, Who with God the Father and the Holy Spirit livest and reignest one God, world without end. Amen.[239]

SACRAMENT OF THE
HOLY EUCHARIST NOVENA

I thank You, Jesus, my Divine Redeemer, for coming upon the earth for our sake, and for instituting the adorable Sacrament of the Holy Eucharist in order to remain with us until the end of the world. I thank You for hiding beneath the Eucharistic Species Your infinite majesty and beauty, which Your angels delight to behold, so that I may have courage to approach the throne of Your Mercy.

I thank You, most loving Jesus, for having made Yourself my food, and for uniting Yourself to me with so much love in this wonderful Sacrament that I may live with You.

I thank You, my Jesus, for giving Yourself to me in this Blessed Sacrament, and so enriching it with the treasure of Your love that You have no greater gift to give me. I thank You not only for having become my food but also for offering Yourself as a continual sacrifice to Your Eternal Father for my salvation.

I thank You, Divine Priest, for offering Yourself as a sacrifice daily upon our altars in adoration and homage to the Most Blessed Trinity, and for making amends for our poor and miserable adorations. I thank You for renewing in this daily Sacrifice the actual Sacrifice of the Cross offered on Calvary, in which You satisfy Divine justice for us poor sinners.

I thank You, dear Jesus, for having become the

priceless Victim to merit for me the fullness of heavenly favors. Awaken in me such confidence in You that their fullness may descend ever more fruitfully upon my soul. I thank You for offering Yourself in thanksgiving to God for all His benefits, spiritual and temporal, which He has bestowed upon me.

In union with Your offering of Yourself to Your Father in the Holy Sacrifice of the Mass, I ask for this special favor: (*Mention your request*).

If it be Your holy Will, grant my request. Through You I also hope to receive the grace of perseverance in Your love and faithful service, a holy death, and a happy eternity with You in heaven. Amen.[240]

NOVENA OF HOLY COMMUNIONS
(For either nine days or nine Sundays)

Jesus, my Eucharistic Friend, accept this Novena of Holy Communions which I am making in order to draw closer to Your Sacred Heart in sincerest love. If it be Your holy Will, grant the special favor for which I am making this novena: (*Mention your request*).

Jesus, You have said, "Ask and it will be given to you; seek and you will find; knock and the door will be opened to you" (Mt 7:7). Through the intercession of Your most holy Mother, Our Lady of the Blessed Sacrament, I ask, I seek, I knock; please grant my prayer.

Jesus, You have said, "Whatever you ask the Father

in my name he will give you" (Jn 16:23). Through the intercession of Your most holy Mother, Our Lady of the Blessed Sacrament, I ask the Father in Your Name to grant my prayer.

Jesus, You have said, "If you ask anything of me in my name, I will do it" (Jn 14:14). Through the intercession of Your most holy Mother, Our Lady of the Blessed Sacrament, I ask in Your Name to grant my prayer.

Jesus, You have said, "If you remain in me and my words remain in you, ask for whatever you want and it will be done for you" (Jn 15:7). Through the intercession of Your most holy Mother, Our Lady of the Blessed Sacrament, may my request be granted, for I wish to live in You through frequent Holy Communion.

Lord, I believe that I can do nothing better in order to obtain the favor I desire than to attend Holy Mass and to unite myself in Holy Communion most intimately with You, the Source of all graces. When You are really and truly present in my soul as God and Man, my confidence is greatest, for You want to help me, because You are all good; You know how to help me, because You are all-wise; You can help me, because You are all-powerful. Most Sacred Heart of Jesus, I believe in Your love for me!

Jesus, as proof of my sincerest gratitude, I promise to receive You in Holy Communion as often as I am able to do so—at every Mass I attend, if possible. Help me to love You in the Holy Eucharist as my greatest

Treasure upon earth. May the effects of frequent Holy Communion help me to serve You faithfully so that I may save my soul and be with You forever in heaven. Amen.[241]

Exposition and Benediction

EXPOSITION: After the people have assembled, a suitable song may be sung (e.g., "O Salutaris") while the celebrant comes to the altar with the Eucharist.

O SALUTARIS HOSTIA

(Victim Saving us from Sin)

O salutaris Hostia,
Quae caeli pandis ostium:
Bella premunt hostilia,
Da robur, fer auxilium.

Uni trinoque Domino
Sit sempiterna gloria,
Qui vitam sine termino
Nobis donet in patria. Amen.

O victim, saving us from sin,
Who opens heaven's gates to us,
From Satan now temptations come,
   Give strength and bring us health.

To You, one God in Persons Three,
We offer everlasting praise,
Who'll give us life that never ends,
   In heaven our homeland true.

After exposition, the celebrant incenses the Sacrament. If the adoration is to be lengthy, he may then withdraw.

ADORATION: During the exposition there should be prayers, songs, readings from Scripture, and a brief homily to direct the attention of the faithful to the worship of the Lord.

BENEDICTION: Toward the end of the exposition the priest or deacon goes to the altar, genuflects, and kneels. A suitable Eucharistic song is sung (e.g., "Tantum Ergo").

TANTUM ERGO

Tantum ergo Sacramentum
    Veneremur cernui:
Et antiquum documentum
    Novo cedat ritui:
Praestet fides supplementum
    Sensuum defectui.

Genitori, Genitoque
    Laus et jubilatio,
Salus, honor, virtus, quoque
    Sit et benedictio:
Procedenti ab utroque
    Compar sit laudatio. Amen.

Down in adoration falling,
This great Sacrament we hail;
Over forms of ancient worship
Newer rites of grace prevail;
Faith will tell us Christ is present,
When our human senses fail.

To the everlasting Father,
And the Son who made us free,
And the Spirit, God proceeding
From them Each eternally,
Be salvation, honor, blessing,
Might and endless majesty. Amen.

PRIEST/DEACON: You have given them Bread from Heaven

ALL: *Having all sweetness within it.* (*Alleluia.*)

PRIEST/DEACON: Lord Jesus Christ, you gave us the Eucharist as a memorial of your suffering and death. May our worship of this Sacrament of your Body and Blood help us to experience the salvation you won for us and the peace of the kingdom where you live with the Father and the Holy Spirit, one God, for ever and ever.

ALL: *Amen.*

The celebrant then blesses the people with the Eucharist.

REPOSITION: After the blessing the priest or deacon replaces the Blessed Sacrament in the tabernacle and genuflects. The following acclamation may be said at this time.

DIVINE PRAISES

Blessed be God.
Blessed be His Holy Name.
Blessed be Jesus Christ, true God and true Man.
Blessed be the Name of Jesus.
Blessed be His most Sacred Heart.
Blessed be His most Precious Blood.
Blessed be Jesus in the most Holy Sacrament of the Altar.
Blessed be the Holy Spirit, the Paraclete.
Blessed be the great Mother of God, Mary most holy.
Blessed be her holy and Immaculate Conception.
Blessed be her glorious Assumption.
Blessed be the name of Mary, Virgin and Mother.
Blessed be Saint Joseph, her most chaste spouse.
Blessed be God in His angels and in His saints.

As the celebrant leaves, the following or another suitable song may be sung.

HOLY GOD, WE PRAISE THY NAME

Holy God, we praise Thy name;
Lord of all, we bow before Thee;
All on earth Thy scepter claim,
All in heaven above adore Thee.

Infinite Thy vast domain,
Everlasting is Thy reign!

Hark, the loud celestial hymn;
Angel choirs above are raising;
Cherubim and Seraphim,
In unceasing chorus praising,
Fill the heavens with sweet accord;
Holy, holy, holy, Lord!

Classic Catholic Prayers

HOW TO PRAY THE ROSARY

1. Starting with the cross at the end of the beads, make the sign of the cross and pray the Apostles' Creed:

The Apostles' Creed

I believe in God, the Father Almighty, creator of heaven and earth; and in Jesus Christ, His only Son, our Lord; Who was conceived by the Holy Spirit, born of the Virgin Mary, suffered under Pontius Pilate, was crucified, died, and was buried. He descended into hell; the third day He arose again from the dead; He ascended into heaven, sits at the right hand of God, the Father Almighty; from thence He shall come to judge the living and the dead. I believe in the Holy Spirit, the holy Catholic Church, the communion of saints, the forgiveness of sins, the resurrection of the body, and life everlasting. Amen.

2. On the first big bead above the cross, pray the Our Father:

Our Father

Our Father, Who art in heaven, hallowed be Thy name; Thy kingdom come; Thy will be done on earth, as it is in heaven. Give us this day our daily bread; and forgive us our trespasses, as we forgive those who trespass against us; and lead us not into temptation, but deliver us from evil. Amen.

3. On the next three small beads, pray three Hail Marys:

Hail Mary

Hail, Mary, full of grace; the Lord is with thee; blessed art thou among women, and blessed is the fruit of thy womb, Jesus. Holy Mary, Mother of God, pray for us sinners, now and at the hour of our death. Amen.

4. Pray the Glory be:

Glory Be

Glory be to the Father, and to the Son, and to the Holy Spirit. As it was in the beginning, is now, and ever shall be, world without end. Amen.

5. On the first big bead of the circle, announce the first mystery;* then pray the Our Father.

6. Pray ten Hail Marys while meditating on the mystery.

7. Pray the Glory be.

8. After each decade pray the following prayer requested by the Blessed Virgin Mary when she appeared at Fatima:

O my Jesus, forgive us our sins, save us from the fires of hell, and lead all souls to heaven, especially those who have most need of thy mercy.

---

* See page 216.

9. Announce the second mystery; then pray the Our Father; repeat nos. 6, 7, and 8 above, and continue with the third, fourth, and fifth mysteries in the same manner.

10. Pray the Hail, Holy Queen after the five decades are completed:

Hail, Holy Queen

Hail, Holy Queen, Mother of Mercy, our life, our sweetness and our hope, to thee do we cry, poor banished children of Eve; to thee do we send up our sighs, mourning and weeping in this vale of tears; turn, then, most gracious Advocate, thine eyes of mercy toward us, and after this, our exile, show unto us the blessed fruit of thy womb, Jesus. O clement, O loving, O sweet Virgin Mary!

Pray for us, O holy Mother of God, that we may be made worthy of the promises of Christ.

11. You may want to add the following prayer:

O God, whose only begotten Son, by His life, death, and resurrection, has purchased for us the rewards of eternal life, grant, we beseech you, that, by meditating on these mysteries in the most Holy Rosary of the Blessed Virgin Mary, we may imitate what they contain and obtain what they promise. Through the same Christ, our Lord. Amen.

* The mysteries of the Rosary are divided into three sets of five:

I. *The Joyful Mysteries*

1. The Annunciation of Our Lord
2. The Visitation
3. The Nativity of Jesus
4. The Presentation of Jesus in the Temple
5. The Finding in the Temple

II. *The Sorrowful Mysteries*

1. The Agony in the Garden
2. The Scourging at the Pillar
3. The Crowning with Thorns
4. The Carrying of the Cross
5. The Crucifixion and Death

III. *The Glorious Mysteries*

1. The Resurrection of Our Lord
2. The Ascension of Christ into Heaven
3. The Descent of the Holy Spirit
4. The Assumption of Mary
5. The Coronation of Mary as Queen of Heaven and Earth

As a general rule, the Joyful Mysteries are said on Mondays and Thursdays, the Sorrowful Mysteries on Tuesday and Friday; the Glorious Mysteries on Wednesday and Saturday. On Sundays the Glorious Mysteries can be prayed. The Joyful Mysteries can be prayed during the Sundays of Advent and the Sorrowful Mysteries on the Sundays in Lent.

HOW TO RECITE THE CHAPLET OF MERCY

The Chaplet of Mercy is recited using ordinary rosary beads of five decades. At the Shrine of the Divine Mercy in Stockbridge, Massachusetts, the Chaplet is preceded by two opening prayers from the *Diary* of Blessed Faustina and followed by a closing prayer.

Optional Opening Prayers

You expired, Jesus, but the source of life gushed forth for souls, and the ocean of mercy opened up for the whole world. O Fount of Life, unfathomable Divine Mercy, envelop the whole world and empty Yourself out upon us (*Diary*, 1319).

O Blood and Water, which gushed forth from the Heart of Jesus as a fountain of Mercy for us, I trust in You! (*Diary*, 84).

Begin the Chaplet with the Our Father, the Hail Mary and the Apostles' Creed.

Then, on the large bead before each decade:

> Eternal Father,
> I offer You the Body and Blood,
> Soul and Divinity of Your dearly Beloved Son,
> Our Lord, Jesus Christ,
> in atonement for our sins
> and those of the whole world.

On the ten small beads of each decade, pray:

> For the sake of His sorrowful Passion,
> have mercy on us and on the whole world.

Conclude with:

> Holy God,
> Holy Mighty One,
> Holy Immortal One,
> have mercy on us
> and on the whole world (*Diary*, 476).

Optional Closing Prayer

Eternal God, in whom mercy is endless and the trea-sury of compassion inexhaustible, look kindly upon us and increase Your mercy in us, that in difficult mo-ments we might not despair nor become despondent, but with great confidence submit ourselves to Your holy will, which is Love and Mercy itself (*Diary*, 950).

THE MEMORARE

Remember, O most gracious Virgin Mary, that never was it known that anyone who fled to thy protection, implored thy help, or sought thy intercession was left unaided. Inspired with this confidence, we fly unto thee, O Virgin of virgins, our Mother; to thee we come; before thee we stand, sinful and sorrowful. O Mother of the Word Incarnate, despise not our petitions, but in thy mercy hear and answer us.

THE ANGELUS

℣. The Angel of the Lord declared unto Mary.
℟. *And she conceived of the Holy Spirit.*

(Hail Mary)

℣. Behold the handmaid of the Lord.
℟. *May it be done unto me according to Your Word.*

(Hail Mary)

℣. And the Word was made flesh. (*Bow slightly here.*)
℟. *And dwelt among us.*

(Hail Mary)

Let us pray:

Pour forth, we beseech Thee, O Lord, Thy grace into our hearts, that we to whom the Incarnation of Christ, Thy Son, was made known by the message of an angel, may by His Passion and Cross be brought to the glory of His Resurrection, through the same Christ, Our Lord. Amen.

AGNUS DEI

Agnus Dei
   qui tollis peccata mundi:
   miserere nobis.
Agnus Dei
   qui tollis peccata mundi:
   miserere nobis.
Agnus Dei
   qui tollis peccata mundi:
   dona nobis pacem.

PRAYER TO SAINT MICHAEL

Saint Michael the Archangel, defend us in battle, be our protection against the wickedness and snares of the devil; may God rebuke him, we humbly pray, and do thou, O Prince of the heavenly host, by the power of God, thrust into hell Satan and all evil spirits, who wander through the world for the ruin of souls. Amen.

PRAYER OF SAINT IGNATIUS

Take, O Lord, and receive all my liberty,
my memory, my understanding,
and my entire will,
all that I have and possess.
You have given to me,
to You, O Lord, I return it.
All is Yours; dispose of it wholly according to Your
    will.
Give me only Your love and Your grace,
for this is enough for me.

PRAYER OF SAINT FRANCIS

Lord make me an instrument of Your peace;
Where there is hatred, let me sow love;
Where there is injury, let me sow pardon;
Where there is discord, let me sow harmony;
Where there is error, let me sow truth.
Where there is doubt, let me sow faith;
Where there is despair, let me sow hope;
Where there is darkness; let me sow light;
Where there is sadness, let me sow joy.
O Divine Master, grant that I may seek
Not so much to be consoled, as to console,
To be understood, as to understand,
To be loved, as to love.
For it is in giving that we receive;

It is in forgiving that we are forgiven;
And it is in dying
That we are born to eternal life.

AN ACT OF FAITH

O my God, I firmly believe that You are one God in three Divine Persons, Father, Son, and Holy Spirit; I believe that Your Divine Son became man and died for our sins, and that He will come to judge the living and the dead. I believe these and all the truths which the holy Catholic Church teaches, because You have revealed them, O Lord, Who can neither deceive nor be deceived.

AN ACT OF HOPE

O my God, relying on Your infinite goodness and promises, I hope to obtain pardon of my sins, the help of Your grace, and life everlasting, through the merits of Jesus Christ, my Lord and Redeemer.

AN ACT OF LOVE

O my God, I love You above all things, with my whole heart and soul, because You are all good and worthy of all love. I love my neighbor as myself for love of You. I forgive all who have injured me, and I ask pardon of all whom I have injured.

I BELIEVE IN THEE

I believe in Thee, I hope in Thee, I love Thee, I adore Thee, O Blessed Trinity, one God; have mercy on me now and at the hour of my death and save me. Amen.

WE ADORE THEE

We adore Thee, most holy Lord Jesus Christ, here and in all Thy churches that are in the whole world, and we bless Thee; because by Thy Holy Cross Thou hast redeemed the World. Amen.

AN ACT OF CONTRITION

O my God, I am heartily sorry for having offended Thee, and I detest all of my sins, because of Thy just punishment, but mostly because they have offended Thee, my God, who art all-good and deserving of all my love. I firmly resolve, with the help of Thy grace, to sin no more and to avoid the near occasions of sin.

I CONFESS (CONFITEOR)

I confess to almighty God, to blessed Mary ever Virgin, to blessed Michael the archangel, to blessed John the Baptist, to the holy apostles Peter and Paul, to all the saints, and to you my brothers and sisters (and to thee, father) that I have sinned exceedingly in thought, word, and deed, through my fault, through my fault, through my most grievous fault. Therefore, I beseech blessed Mary ever Virgin, blessed Michael the archangel, blessed John the Baptist, the holy apostles Peter and Paul, and all the saints, to pray for me to the Lord our God. Amen.

I confess to Almighty God and to you, brethren, that I have sinned exceedingly in thought, word, deed, and omission, through my fault, through my fault, through my most grievous fault. Therefore I beg blessed Mary ever Virgin, all the Angels and Saints, and you, brethren, to pray for me to the Lord our God. Amen.

DE PROFUNDIS

Out of the depths, I cry to You, O Lord, Lord, listen to my voice; let but Your ears be attentive to the voice that calls to You for pardon.

If You, Lord, will keep account of our iniquities, Master who has the strength to bear it? Ah! but with You there is forgiveness, be Your name ever revered. I wait for the Lord. For His word of promise, my soul waits, patient as a watchman that looked for the day, patient as a watchman at dawn for the Lord; let Israel wait for the Lord with whom there is forgiveness, the Lord with whom there is power and ransom.

He it is that will ransom Israel from all his iniquities.

PRAYER BEFORE A CRUCIFIX

Behold, O good and most sweet Jesus, I fall upon my knees before Thee, and with most fervent desire beg and beseech Thee that Thou wouldst impress upon my heart a lively sense of faith, hope and charity, true repentance for my sins, and a firm resolve to make amends. And with deep affection and grief, I reflect upon Thy five wounds, having before my eyes that which Thy prophet David spoke about Thee, O good Jesus: "They have pierced my hands and feet, they have counted all my bones."

Amen.

COME, HOLY GHOST, CREATOR BLEST

Come, Holy Ghost, Creator blest,
and in our souls take up Thy rest;
come with Thy grace and heavenly aid,
to fill the hearts which Thou hast made.

O comforter, to Thee we cry,
O heavenly gift of God Most High,
O fount of life and fire of love,
and sweet anointing from above.

Thou in Thy sevenfold gifts are known;
Thou, finger of God's hand we own;
Thou, promise of the Father, Thou
Who dost the tongue with power imbue.

Kindle our senses from above,
and make our hearts o'erflow with love;
with patience firm and virtue high
the weakness of our flesh supply.

Far from us drive the foe we dread,
and grant us Thy peace instead;
so shall we not, with Thee for guide,
turn from the path of life aside.

Oh, may Thy grace on us bestow
the Father and the Son to know;
and Thee, through endless times confessed,
of both the eternal Spirit blest.

Now to the Father and the Son,
Who rose from death, be glory given,
with Thou, O Holy Comforter,
henceforth by all in earth and heaven.
Amen.

COME, HOLY SPIRIT

Come, Holy Spirit, fill the hearts of Thy faithful and
kindle in them the fire of Thy love.
Send forth Thy Spirit and they shall be created;
And Thou shalt renew the face of the earth. Amen.

Let us pray:

O God, Who didst teach the hearts of Thy faithful
people by sending them the light of the Holy Spirit,

grant us by the same Spirit, to have a right judgment in all things, and evermore rejoice in His holy comfort. Through Christ our Lord. Amen.

TAKE FROM ME
MY HEART OF STONE

O Lord, take away my heart of stone, my hardened heart, my uncircumcised heart, and grant to me a new heart, a heart of flesh, a clean heart! O Thou who purifieth the heart and loveth the clean heart, possess my heart and dwell in it, containing it and filling it, higher than my highest and more intimate than my most intimate thoughts. Thou who art the image of all beauty and the seal of all holiness, seal my heart in Thine image and seal my heart in Thy mercy, O God of my heart and the God of my portion in eternity. Amen.

MORNING OFFERING

O Jesus, through the Immaculate Heart of Mary, I offer You all my prayers, works, joys, and sufferings of this day, for all the intentions of Your Sacred Heart, in union with the Holy Sacrifice of the Mass throughout the world, in reparation for my sins, for the intentions of all our associates, and for the general intention recommended by the Holy Father this month.

GLORY TO GOD

Glory to God in the Highest and peace on earth to men of goodwill. We praise you, we bless you, we adore you, we glorify you, we give you thanks for your great glory. O Lord God, heavenly King, God the Father Almighty. Lord Jesus Christ, the only-begotten Son, Lord God, Lamb of God, Son of the Father, you take away the sins of the world; have mercy on us. You take away the sins of the world: receive our prayer. You are seated at the right hand of the Father: have mercy on us. For you alone are the Holy One, you alone are the Lord, you alone are the Most High, O Jesus Christ, with the Holy Spirit, in the glory of God the Father. Amen.

TE DEUM

O God, we praise Thee and acknowledge Thee to be
   the supreme Lord.
Everlasting Father, all the earth worships Thee.
All the Angels, the heavens and all angelic powers,
All the Cherubim and Seraphim, continuously cry
   to Thee:
Holy, Holy, Holy, Lord God of Hosts!
Heaven and earth are full of the Majesty of Thy glory.
The glorious choir of the Apostles,
The wonderful company of Prophets,
The white-robed army of Martyrs praise Thee.

Holy Church throughout the world acknowledges
    Thee:
The Father of infinite Majesty;
Thy adorable, true and only Son;
Also the Holy Spirit, the Comforter.
O Christ, Thou art the King of glory!
Thou art the everlasting Son of the Father.
When Thou tookest it upon Thyself to deliver man,
Thou didst not disdain the Virgin's womb.
Having overcome the sting of death, Thou opened the
Kingdom of Heaven to all believers.
Thou sittest at the right hand of God in the glory of
    the Father.
We believe that Thou wilt come to be our Judge.
We, therefore, beg Thee to help Thy servants whom
    Thou hast redeemed with Thy Precious Blood.
Let them be numbered with Thy Saints in everlasting
    glory.

℣. Save Thy people, O Lord, and bless Thine
    inheritance!
℟. *Govern them, and raise them up forever.*
℣. Every day we thank Thee.
℟. *And we praise Thy Name forever, yes, forever and ever.*
℣. O Lord, deign to keep us from sin this day.
℟. *Have mercy on us, O Lord, have mercy on us.*
℣. Let Thy mercy, O Lord, be upon us, for we have
    hoped in Thee.
℟. *O Lord, in Thee I have put my trust; let me never be
    put to shame.*

NOTES

[1] Lk 22:7–20. Scripture citations are taken from *The Holy Bible, Containing the Old and New Testaments, Revised Standard Version, Catholic Edition* (San Francisco: Ignatius Press, 1995, including the Catholic edition of the New Testament, copyright 1965, the Catholic edition of the Old Testament incorporating the Apocrypha, copyright 1966, by the Division of Christian Education of the National Council of the Churches of Christ in the United States of America).

[2] Mk 14:22–24.

[3] Mt 26:26–28.

[4] Jn 6:25–70.

[5] Lk 24:28–35.

[6] Mt 5:23–24.

[7] 1 Cor 10:16–17.

[8] 1 Cor 11:17–34.

[9] Ex 12:21–27.

[10] Ex 12:1–8.

[11] Ex 16:2–4, 31–35.

[12] Saint Ignatius of Antioch, *Letter to the Ephesians* 13, in *The Early Christian Fathers*, ed. Henry Bettenson (Oxford and New York: Oxford University Press, 1984), 40.

[13] Saint Ignatius of Antioch, *Letter to the Ephesians* 12–20, in ibid., 45.

[14] Saint Ignatius of Antioch, *Letter to the Romans* 4–7, in ibid., 47.

[15] Saint Ignatius of Antioch, *Letter to the Philadelphians* 4 in ibid.

[16] Saint Ignatius of Antioch, *Letter to the Smyrnaeans* 6, in ibid., 48.

[17] Saint Ignatius of Antioch, *Letter to the Smyrnaeans* 8, in ibid., 49.

[18] *The Didachē* 9, in ibid., 51.

[19] *The Didachē* 14, in ibid., 52.

[20] Saint Justin Martyr, *Apologia* 1, 65–66, in ibid., 61.

[21] Ibid., 62.

[22] Saint Irenaeus of Lyons, *Against Heresies* 4, 17–18, in ibid., 94.

[23] Ibid., 95.

[24] Ibid.

[25] Saint Irenaeus of Lyons, *Against Heresies* 4, 18, 4–6, in ibid., 96.

[26] Ibid., 5, 2, 2–3, in ibid., 97.

[27] Melito of Sardis, "Paschal Homily", in *The Mass: Ancient Liturgies and Patristic Texts*, ed. Adalbert Hamman (Staten Island, N.Y.: Alba House, 1969), 79.

[28] Tertullian, *De Resurrectione Carnis* 8, in Bettenson, *Early Christian Fathers*, 148.

[29] Tertullian, *De Oratione* 19, in ibid., 149.

[30] Saint Cyprian of Carthage, *Letter* 63, Cyprian to Brother Cecil, in *The Early Christian Fathers*, ed. Henry Bettenson (Oxford and New York: Oxford University Press, 1984), 272.

[31] Ibid.

[32] Ibid.

[33] Saint Athanasius, *Epistolae Festales* 4, 3, in ibid., 298.

[34] Saint John Chrysostom, *Homily* 82, on Matthew 26:26–28, in Hamman, *The Mass*, 94.

[35] Ibid., 102.

[36] Ibid.

[37] Ibid., 103.

[38] Ibid., 104.

[39] Saint John Chrysostom, *Homily* 46, on John 6:41–53, in ibid., 113.

[40] Ibid.

[41] Ibid., 114.

[42] Ibid., 115.

[43] Saint John Chrysostom, *Homily* 24, on 1 Corinthians, in ibid., 157.

[44] Ibid., 158.

[45] Ibid., 162.

[46] Ibid.

[47] Ibid., 164.

[48] Ibid., 165.

[49] Saint Cyril of Jerusalem, *Catechetical Lectures* 23.15, in Bettenson, *Later Christian Fathers*, 46.

[50] Ibid., 45.

[51] Saint Hilary of Poitiers, *De Trinitate*, 8, 13–17, in ibid., 57.

[52] Ibid.

[53] Ibid., 58.

[54] Saint Gregory of Nazianzus, *Funebris in Luaden Sororis* 8, 18, in ibid., 123.

[55] Saint Gregory of Nazianzus, *Funebris in Luaden Sororis* 171, in ibid., 124.

[56] Saint Gregory of Nyssa, *Oratio Catechetica* 37, in ibid., 162.

[57] Saint Ambrose, *De Mysteriis*, 52–54, in ibid., 185.

[58] Saint Ambrose, *Expositio in Psalmum* 38, 25, in ibid., 186.

[59] Saint Augustine of Hippo, *Sermon* 227, To Neophytes, on the Sacred Mystery, in Hamman, *The Mass*, 205.

[60] Saint Augustine of Hippo, *Sermon* 329, On the Feast of a Martyr, 1, in ibid., 209.

[61] Saint Augustine of Hippo, *Sermon on the Sacrament of the Altar—Sermon Denys* 3, in ibid., 210.

[62] Saint Augustine of Hippo, *Sermon on the Day of Easter* 1, in ibid., 219.

[63] Ibid.

[64] Ibid.

[65] Saint Augustine of Hippo, *De Civitate Dei* 10, 5, 6, in ibid., 244.

[66] Saint Augustine of Hippo, *De Baptismo Contra Donatistas* 5, 9, in ibid., 246.

[67] Saint Augustine of Hippo, *Enarrationes in Psalmos* 98, 9, in ibid., 247.

[68] Saint Augustine of Hippo, *Sermon* 130, in Hamman, *The Mass*, 210.

[69] Saint Augustine of Hippo, *In Evangelium Johannis Tractatus*, 21, 8, in Bettenson, *Later Christian Fathers*, 248.

[70] Saint Cyril of Alexandria, *In Lucam* 22, 19, in ibid., 268.

[71] Saint Cyril of Alexandria, *Commentary on Saint John* 4, 2 and 3, in ibid., 269.

[72] Saint Faustus of Riez, *A Homily on the Body and Blood of Christ* 1, in Hamman, *The Mass*, 234.

[73] Ibid.

[74] Ibid., 239.

[75] Saint Caesarius of Arles, *Sermon* 227, On the Consecration of the Altar, 2–3, in ibid., 241.

[76] Saint John of Damascus, *De Fide Orthodoxa*, PG 94, in ibid., 269.

[77] Ibid.

[78] Stephen, Bishop of Autun, *Tractatus de Sacramento Altaris* 172, in ibid., 281.

[79] Lateran Council IV, DS 802.

[80] Saint Francis of Assisi, *Second Letter—Letter to All Clerics*.

[81] Ibid.

[82] Saint Clare of Assisi, *Letters*.

[83] Saint Thomas Aquinas, *De Articulis Fidei et Sacramentis Ecclesiae* 2, in *Saint Thomas Aquinas: Theological Texts*, ed. Thomas Gilby (Oxford and New York: Oxford University Press, 1982), 351.

[84] Ibid.

[85] Saint Thomas, *IV Contra Gentes*, 56, in ibid., 354.

[86] Ibid.

[87] Saint Thomas, *Disputations, XXVII de Veritate* 4, in ibid., 356.

[88] Saint Thomas, *Maundy Thursday Sermon*, in ibid., 364.

[89] Saint Thomas, *Breviary Lessons, Corpus Christi*, in ibid., 365.

[90] Ibid., 366.

[91] Ibid.

[92] Saint Thomas, *IV Sentences*, 10, 1, in ibid., 368.

[93] Saint Thomas, *Summa Theologica*, 3a, 75, 1, in ibid., 368.

[94] Ibid.

[95] Ibid., 369.

[96] Ibid.

[97] Saint Thomas, *IV Sentences*, 13, 3, 1, 4, in ibid., 373.

[98] Urban IV, *Transiturus*, in James O'Connor, *The Hidden Manna* (San Francisco: Ignatius Press, 1988), 192.

[99] Saint Catherine of Siena, *The Dialogue*, 128.

[100] Thomas à Kempis, *The Imitation of Christ*, bk. 4, chap. 1.

[101] *The Council of Trent*, DS 1740.

[102] Ibid., DS 1743.

[103] Ibid., DS 1651.

[104] Ibid., DS 1642.

[105] Ibid.

[106] Ibid., DS 16.

[107] Saint Teresa of Jesus, *The Way of Perfection*, chap. 35, in *The Complete Works of Saint Teresa of Jesus*, ed. E. A. Peers (London: Sheed and Ward, 1972), 111.

[108] Saint Teresa of Jesus, in *The Way of Perfection*, chap. 34, in ibid.

[109] Saint Robert Bellarmine, *De Missa* 1, chap. 2.

[110] Saint Margaret Mary, *Letters of Saint Margaret Mary* (Orlando: Men of the Sacred Heart, 1976), Letter 56.

[111] Saint Margaret Mary, ibid., Letter 5.

[112] Saint Louis de Montfort, *True Devotion to the Blessed Virgin* (Bay Shore, N.Y.: Montfort Publications, 1991), 136–40.

[113] Saint Alphonsus de Liguori, *The Holy Eucharist* (Brooklyn, N.Y.: Redemptorist Fathers, 1934), 74.

[114] Ibid., 87.

[115] Ibid., 117.

[116] Ibid., 118.

[117] Ibid., 148.

[118] Saint John Vianney, "Sermon for Holy Thursday", in *Eucharistic Meditations*, ed. Sr. Mary Benvenuta, O.P., trans. Abbé H. Convert (Trabuco Canyon, Calif.: Source Books, 1993), 32.

[119] Ibid.

[120] Saint John Vianney, "Esprit", in ibid., 35.

[121] Ibid., 46.

[122] Ibid., 57.

[123] Ibid., 62.

[124] Saint John Vianney, *Sermons* 2, 245, in ibid., 72.

[125] Saint John Vianney, "Esprit", in ibid., 77.

[126] Saint John Vianney, *Sermons* 2, in ibid., 246.

[127] Saint John Vianney, "Esprit", in ibid., 89.

[128] Ibid., 91.

[129] Saint John Vianney, *Sermons* 2, 137–38, in ibid., 112.

[130] Saint John Vianney, in ibid., 116.

[131] Saint Peter Julian Eymard, in *Eucharistic Handbook* (Cleveland, Ohio: Emmanuel Publications, 1948), 27.

[132] Ibid., 30.

[133] Ibid., 42.

[134] Ibid., 27.

[135] Ibid., 56.

[136] Ibid., 61.

[137] Ibid., 62.

[138] Ibid., 64.

[139] John Henry Cardinal Newman, "Loss and Gain, the Story of a Convert", in *John Henry Cardinal Newman: The Mystery of the Church*, ed. M. K. Strolz et al. (Rome: Centre of Newman Friends, 1981), 45.

[140] John Henry Cardinal Newman, "The Eucharistic Presence", *Parochial and Plain Sermons*, vol. 6 (San Francisco: Ignatius Press, 1997), 1281.

[141] Cardinal Newman, "Infant Baptism", *Parochial and Plain Sermons*, vol. 3, in ibid., 667.

[142] Cardinal Newman, "Reverence in Worship", *Parochial and Plain Sermons*, vol. 8, in ibid., 1571.

[143] Cardinal Newman, "Lectures on the Present Position of Catholics in England" in *John Henry Cardinal Newman*, ed. Strolz et al., 68.

[144] Pope Leo XIII, *Mirae Caritatis*, 7, *Acta Leonis* XIII, in *The Papal Encyclicals, 1878–1903*, ed. Claudia Carlen, IHM (Ann Arbor, Mich.: Pierian Press, 1990), 502.

[145] Ibid., 505.

[146] Sr. Faustina Kowalska, *Divine Mercy in My Soul: Diary of Sr. Faustina*, (Stockbridge, Mass.: Marian Press, 1987), 347.

[147] Ibid., 442.

[148] Ibid., 914.

[149] Ibid., 1385.

[150] Ibid., 145.

[151] Pope Pius XI, "On Reparation Due to the Sacred Heart", 1.

[152] Pope Pius XII, *Mystici Corporis Christi*, 35.

[153] Pope Pius XII, *Mediator Dei*, 39.

[154] Blessed Josemaría Escrivá, *The Way* (Princeton, N.J.: Scepter Publishers, 1982), no. 432, p. 144.

[155] Ibid., no. 531, p. 178.

[156] Ibid., no. 534, p. 179.

[157] Ibid., 535, p. 179.

[158] Ibid., no. 537, p. 180.

[159] Ibid., no. 541, pp. 180–81.

[160] Ibid., no. 322, p. 105.

[161] Ibid., no. 569, pp. 191–92.

[162] Ibid., no. 105, p. 34.

[163] Pope Paul VI, *Mysterium Fidei*.

[164] Ibid.

[165] Ibid.

[166] Ibid.

[167] Ibid.

[168] Ibid.

[169] The Constitution on the Sacred Liturgy, *Sacrosanctum Concilium* (hereafter SC), 5–6, in *Documents of Vatican II*, ed. Austin Flannery (Grand Rapids, Mich.: William B. Eerdmans Publishing Co., 1984), 3–4.

[170] SC 7, in ibid., 4–5.

[171] SC 10, in ibid., 6.

[172] SC 47, in ibid., 16.

[173] On Holy Communion and the Worship of the Eucharistic Mystery Outside of Mass, *Eucharistiae Sacramentum*, 25, in ibid., 249.

[174] Instruction on the Worship of the Eucharistic Mystery, *Eucharisticum Mysterium* (hereafter EM), 1B, in ibid., 106–7.

[175] EM 1D, in ibid., 108.

[176] EM 1E, in ibid., 109.

[177] Dogmatic Constitution on the Church, *Lumen Gentium*, 3, in ibid., 351.

[178] Apostolic Exhortation on the Renewal of Religious Life, *Evangelico Testificatio*, 48, in ibid., 702.

[179] EM, intro., B, in ibid., 101.

[180] EM 1, I, in ibid., 111–12.

181 Ibid., 112, quoting the Decree on the Ministry and Life of Priests, 6.

182 EM, intro., C, 1, in ibid., 102.

183 Ibid.

184 EM, intro., C, 2, in ibid., 102–3.

185 EM, intro., C, 3, in ibid., 103.

186 EM, intro., C, 5, in ibid., 103–4.

187 Ibid., 104.

188 EM, intro., C, 6–7, in ibid.

189 EM, 3, 1, B, in ibid., 129–130.

190 Mother Teresa, *One Heart Full of Love* (Ann Arbor, Mich.: Servant Publications, 1984), 3.

191 Ibid., 6.

192 Mother Teresa, *Mother Teresa: Total Surrender*, ed. Brother Angelo Devananda (Ann Arbor, Mich.: Servant Publications, 1985), 21.

193 Ibid., 21.

194 Ibid., 22.

195 Ibid., 23.

196 Ibid., 24.

197 Ibid., 25.

198 Ibid., 26.

199 Ibid.

200 Ibid., 27.

201 Canon 840, *The Code of Canon Law* (Vatican City: Libreria Editrice Vaticana, 1983).

202 Canon 897, ibid.

203 Canon 898, ibid.

204 Pope John Paul II, *Dominicae Cenae*, 2.

205 Ibid., 3.

206 Ibid.

207 Ibid., 6.

208 Ibid., 7.

[209] Ibid.

[210] Ibid., 8.

[211] Ibid., 9.

[212] Ibid.

[213] Ibid., 3.

[214] Martin Lucia, SS.CC., *Loving Jesus with the Heart of Mary* (*Fifteen Eucharistic Meditations on the Fifteen Mysteries of the Rosary*), (West Covina, Calif.: Eucharistic Adoration, 1985), 1.

[215] Ibid., 2.

[216] Ibid.

[217] Ibid., 4.

[218] *Catechism of the Catholic Church* (Washington, D.C.: United States Catholic Conference, 1994), 1325 (hereafter CCC).

[219] CCC 1326.

[220] CCC 1327.

[221] CCC 1328.

[222] CCC 1329.

[223] CCC 1330.

[224] CCC 1331.

[225] CCC 1332.

[226] CCC 1359.

[227] CCC 1360.

[228] CCC 1361.

[229] *The Raccolta or a Manual of Indulgences*, ed. J. P. Christopher, C. E. Spence, J. F. Rowan (New York, N.Y.: Benzinger Brothers, 1952), p. 96.

[230] Ibid., no. 184, p. 122.

[231] Ibid., no. 163, pp. 94–95.

[232] Ibid., no. 181, p. 119.

[233] A. J. Paone, *My Daily Bread* (Brooklyn, N.Y.: Confraternity of the Precious Blood, 1954), 393–95.

[234] Ibid., 395–98.

[235] Christopher, et al., *Raccolta*, no. 178, pp. 113–16.

[236] *A Prayerbook of Favorite Litanies*, ed. Herbert Albert (Rockford, Ill.: Tan Books and Publishers, 1985), 23–24.

[237] Ibid., 43–45.

[238] Ibid., 46–49.

[239] Ibid., 50–52.

[240] *Treasury of Novenas*, ed. Lawrence Lovasik, S.V.D. (New York, N.Y.: Catholic Book Publishing Co., 1986), 133.

[241] Ibid., 140.

Index

Documents

Saints and Other Persons

Prayers